WRO

A life of purpose and selfless service to God

An Autobiography of
William Rufus Olatunji Ojo

FIGHT!
By Revd. Dr. William Rufus Olatunji Ojo
Copyright © 2020 by Revd. Dr William Rufus Olatunji Ojo

FIGHT!
ISBN: 978-1-908-015-09-9

All rights reserved under the International Copyright Law. The author guarantees all contents are original and do not infringe upon the legal rights of any other person or work. No part of this publication may be reproduced, stored in a retrieval system, or transmitted in any form or by any means, electronic, mechanical, photocopying, recording or otherwise, without the prior written permission of Protokos Publishers and GWF (Grace William Foundation).
Unless otherwise stated, all scripture quotations in this book are taken from the New King James Version of The Holy Bible.

Published by,
Protokos Publishers for GWF
Website: https://protokospublishersonline.com
Email: info@protokospublishersonline.com
Tel: +44 7944 697 977

GWF (Grace William Foundation)
Plot 319, Odusami Street,
Ogba-Aguda,
Lagos, Nigeria.
Tel: +234 802 312 7082

Cover design and illustrations:
Johnbull Oghenechovwe (Justjohn Associates Ltd)
Photographs from GWF Archives
Layout Design by Redsorel Designs

Dedication

To the glory of God, the Father of all grace, Jesus Christ, the Great Shepherd of the Sheep and the Holy Spirit, our Guide and Comforter, who chose me to be a partaker of the inheritance of the saints in light, and called me with a heavenly calling, who endowed me with long life and zeal to serve in His vineyard and by whose grace I am what I am.

Book review

Rev. Dr. W. R.O. Ojo has left for us a pen photograph of how and what it means to serve God in this world in which we live for a while before we return to our heavenly residence to give account of our services to God who sent us here. No stewardship when we get to heaven.

My plead is that each of us should read Dr. Ojo's account of his stewardship again and again knowing that bye and bye each of us will stand before our creator to give account of how we carried out our responsibility. No one can escape standing before our creator to give account of how he/she carried out his/her responsibilities during our stay on earth as children of God. May God help us not to fail in carrying out our God given responsibilities during our sojourn here. May we all follow the example of our brother Rev. Dr. W. R. O. Ojo who spent his life carrying out his responsibilities during his sojourn on earth, amen.

Rev. Prof. Osadolor Imasogie

Table of Contents

Dedication	v
Book Review	vi
Preface	viii
Acknowledgement	xi

Chapter One:	**Igbara-oke: where it all began!**	1
Chapter Two:	**Passport to knowledge**	18
Chapter Three:	**The call to ministry**	47
Chapter Four:	**Two bodies, one soul**	57
Chapter Five:	**Trials and Triumphs**	73
Chapter Six:	**From station to station**	79
Chapter Seven:	**Across the oceans**	108
Chapter Eight:	**Call to higher duties**	127
Chapter Nine:	**Retired but not tired!**	138
Chapter Ten:	**Sojourner in England**	154

Appendix	168
Other Books by the Author	188

Preface

William Rufus Olatunji Ojo, D. Min

WRO placed a lot of value on his family, not just his immediate family of wife and children, but the larger family of parents, siblings, aunties and uncles, nephews and nieces and of course, grandchildren. Observing his relationship with mum was a study on its own, of how to make marriages work and how to build strong homes. He was faithful to his marital vows until mum breathed her last, which was barely nine months before he passed on also. Their marriage was free from physical and verbal abuse and there was never a time that we saw them exchange hot words. Dad took the interest of his family as first priority. He ensured that we were well catered for, providing us with the necessities of life, even when we were not rich!

As a father, he was doting and was involved in all our life endeavours – from school to work, and to marriage, and when the grandchildren started to come, albeit in the twilight of their lives, not only did he shower them with gifts at every opportunity, he gave of his time also; to teach, to pray and to love them, just as he and mum had done with us! Dad encouraged and prayerfully propelled us all into our destinies and, today, we all, are products of the grace of God and of the tireless efforts of our parents over us.

As a minister of God, dad was unique. His entire life was defined by the word of God and by his faith, a faith that he demonstrated constantly throughout his sojourn on Planet Earth. He taught us that life is a choice and a fight! between good and bad and, fight! he did; for his faith, for his family, for his health, for his life, until every challenging situation became a medley of praise. We are confident therefore, that at the end of his life, as he prayed, that he was able to say like Apostle Paul, "I have fought the good fight of faith..." and now that he has joined the throng of heavenly hosts, he is looking down and urging us on, with only one word on his lips, Fight!

WRO was dedicated to his call and worked tirelessly to see the growth of the church, not only of the physical structures, but of the men and women, and children, from all walks of life, and from every tribe and tongue, who sought Christ and His redeeming grace, through the doors of the Baptist Mission. He was the first Nigerian to become the Sunday School Secretary of the Baptist Convention, a position he held for many years. When the idea of setting up a Baptist University in Nigeria was mooted, he was selected to champion the cause with the duty of raising forty thousand pounds for the project, an assignment that eventually provided the platform for which he was decorated, with an honorary doctorate degree presented by the Bowen University in 2012.

Dad was a great teacher, who ensured that he imparted the lives of anyone he came in contact with, in the course of his life, and he never stopped learning. He had mentors like Pa Agboola, Pa Ladapo and Dr. Dahunsi, to mention a few. At 80 years, he attended the Lewisham College in London, to learn how to use computers. One of the evidences of the knowledge he acquired through this training is this book and a couple of other writings. Dad literally typed the manuscript by himself! A little writing today and a little writing tomorrow, I watched him document his story, sometimes with mum reminding him of dates and people, or jogging his memories about some event or the other.

After the initial editing, and, as we were about to start work on the manuscript, he took ill. Trusting God that he would recover shortly, we deferred work on the book to focus on his health. I made a promise however, that by the grace of God, I would get his autobiography published. Shortly after his home call, as I tidied up his bedroom, I ran into the well-labelled flash drive titled 'autobiography'.

As a family, we are grateful to God for giving dad the grace to document his story in this book, as only very little, if any lessons, can be learnt from an undocumented life. We are indebted also, to our father for painstakingly taking the time to give a detailed account of his life and in a way, our mother's life too.

With a great sense of pride therefore, Protokos Publishers is grateful and privileged to present to you, FIGHT!, in the hope that you will learn a thing or two, from the life of this humble servant of God – a man of integrity, a great visionary and trailblazer.

Oluwakemi Ola-Ojo
Protokos Publishers
March, 2020.

Acknowledgements

"I thank my God every time I remember you."
- Philippians 1:3

Through the grace and mercy of God Almighty and the love, care and moral support of the undermentioned good people, I am what I am today. Thanks be to God!

I am eternally grateful to my heavenly Father for the type of family He gave me. God in His mercy gave me a loving and understanding wife, Grace Modupe, three useful and wonderful sons; Jaiye, Dapo and Supo, and two daughters; Kemi and Remi, with their own families and children. I have been richly blessed by them and I say like Joshua, *"As for me and my house, we will serve the Lord (Joshua 25:14)."*

I cannot but remember my grandmothers (Fatomiye and Famulayo), who lavished much love on me as their first grandson. Chief (Mrs.) Sarah Omowunmi Ogbede, my sister and adopted mother and our parents' oldest child. She was a good leader at home, in the community and the Church. Her investments in my life and immediate family cannot be quantified. I am ever grateful.

There are several people whose paths crossed mine in the journey of life and without whom my story would not be complete. S.O. Akinluyi (headmaster and later Archdeacon), whom God used to convince my father to send me to school in 1934. Chief Ade Komolafe, my best teacher and friend in the primary school. He challenged me to develop and to use diligently, the talents God has given me. I.O.S. Okusanya (Reverend and later Bishop), who taught members of the Boys' Brigade by example, to be honest, disciplined and faithful in all we do. B.A. Falana, Jacob Oyewole, William Obele. The Odeneyes and the Adeoyes opened the doors of their homes to me as a student in Abeokuta. Rev. B.T. Griffin, the High School principal at Baptist Boys High School, Abeokuta, employed me as the first full-time librarian to enable me earn some money to complete my secondary school education.

What shall it profit a man if he gains the whole world and loses his soul? Irrespective of our achievements in life, no matter how great they are, if we lose our souls, all our labour would be in vain. For this reason, I acknowledge the efforts of Reverend J.O. Ajani who led the annual revival service in BBHS, Abeokuta in 1946, where I accepted Jesus Christ as my Lord and Saviour and became born again. On that day, I laid hold of the greatest gift of all and since then, my song has been "I have decided to follow Jesus, No turning back, No turning back."

Dr. J.T. Ayorinde, baptised me in 1946 and became my first Baptist pastor, and later, my mentor. I also served under him when he was General Secretary. He was my father in the Lord and he, with the help of the Holy Spirit, created pathways that made my pastoral journey easy. I am grateful.

I will forever remember with great appreciation, the following mentors for the blessings they brought into my life –P.J. Ladapo, E.A. Dahunsi, E.O. Agboola, Aunty Rachael Famuyiwa, E.L. Akinsanya and friends like

S.A. Lawanson, Dr. Kehinde Anifowose, S.A. Adedeji, A.A. Akinbola, S.S. Ayanda, Chief J.B. Ojo, Rev. Dr. Frank Goveia and many others.

I appreciate especially, our daughter, Kemi, who has continued to defy all odds, to be everything to my wife and I – carer, cook, housekeeper, confidant and all. Many daughters have done excellently but you surpass them all. I rest on her promise to convert this manuscript to a book, in the hope that my story can serve as a navigator to others coming behind me and, also, that those who would read it eventually, would know that I passed this way!

Protokos Publishers would like to thank also, Bolanle Sogunro for her initial efforts in putting the manuscript together.

Finally, we would like to recognise the immense contributions of the editor, `Sumbo Oladipo, for her skills, time, and thoroughness in putting the book together, and for her efforts in making the project a reality in quality time. Thank you for an excellent job!

God bless you all!

CHAPTER ONE

IGBARA-OKE: WHERE IT ALL BEGAN!

"Before I formed you in the womb I knew you, before you were born I set you apart."
- Jeremiah 1:5 (NIV)

I was born in Igbara-Oke, Ondo State of Nigeria, on June 1, 1923 to Gabriel Famadesan, Fatomiye and Leah Adun. I was named William Rufus Olatunji Ojo, Olatunji in honour of my late brother and first son of my parents. The other two names were given to me at baptism. To be baptized in those days, you were either named after some Biblical character or after someone who had achieved greatness and was a person of influence in his lifetime. It is in this regard that I was named William Rufus after one of the great kings who ruled England. In like manner, my elder sister was named Sarah by the church but my parents named her Omowunmi at birth.

My names were chosen by one of the Anglican priests in Igbara-Oke who envisioned that I would be great in life. My parents did not object to any of the names but my father and his family preferred to call me William while my mother's family, stuck to Rufus. The choice of those names would eventually be a prophecy that pointed to the future that I would, indeed, be great. Interestingly, there are people in Igbara-Oke today who still call me William Rufus, the king. Personally, I did not object to being called by any, since both names were mine.

Growing up in those days was a basket of experiences; some good and some not so amusing, yet they all added up to give me a good insight into the pathway that I would eventually tread in life. I grew up under the watchful eyes of my father because of the special affection he had for me. He was the type of man you could call a hands-on father who wanted the best for his children. He was not rich but he made sure we did not lack the basic necessities of life that would have suggested that things were a bit difficult for us because, despite the fact that there were not so many luxuries to enjoy in those days, my family could still be considered to be a middle-class household. Father was a farmer and like other villagers, he embraced it wholeheartedly since it was the main source of income and avenue through which most families could put food on their tables in his time.

My Immediate Family
My mother, Leah Adun, like most women in her days, was a full-time housewife. She was the first wife of my father and must have married at the age of 25 or thereabout. Marriage in those days came with an unwritten requirement: you had to be very strong because it came with many rigours. Mothers had to take care of the children, cook and go to the farm if need be, to assist their husbands. Unfortunately, our mother died suddenly while my sister and I were growing up and her death left a wide gap in the family. Her sudden death was very painful to everyone and because of that, any reminder of it evoked painful emotions that drew tears from everyone in the family, especially my grandmothers.

We lived in a family house with a large compound that sheltered a large number of our family members – immediate and distant. My father had a younger brother and four sisters. He was the first child among the six children from my paternal grandmother. My paternal grandmother, my uncle, Peter Adegoke, four daughters (Aunties Osufo, Asake, Felicia and Dorcas and an uncle, Daniel Obotoye, were some of the people who shared the compound with us and we all lived peaceably without any rancour or quarrel. My sister and I loved our grandmother and Auntie Felicia very much as both were kind to us, giving us food and helping us to wash our clothes. While our parents provided for our needs, we, the young ones, shared the chores of cleaning the compound and making sure everywhere was kept clean but the responsibility to fend for the family fell on the men. They provided the family with food items and every other need. As for my father, he planted yams and cocoa, and, on many occasions, when the work was too much for him and his brothers to do, he hired more hands to assist them during harvest. Being a good family man, he also made sure he brought enough food to the house before he took any leftovers to the market for sale.

I loved going to the farm with father and his brothers because it was always fun to be there. Whenever father and his brothers set out to the farm, I would plead with them to allow me to go along with them because you ate whatever you wanted on the farm. Whenever I went to the farm with them, I enjoyed hunting for rabbits, birds and other animals. I had in my arsenal, a catapult which I was always happy to brandish whenever I was ready for any kill. If only the birds could devise a better way of avoiding being struck down, I would not have been so successful with my strikes but like a combatant at war, I knew how to hide and when to strike and any unfortunate bird that was by my shots ended up roasted and eaten with relish, on the farm. We usually went to the farm on Mondays and returned on Saturday morning, but in case there was so much to do on the farm, we always returned home on Saturday evenings because father always had meetings to attend in the church the following day, being Sunday. He was an Olori-Egbe in the church as well as in the village and, as a result of this, we were compelled to return early in order to prepare for the church service on Sunday.

Until their demise, my paternal grandparents were traditional worshipers who served the deity with enthusiasm, a religion that my parents also practised until the advent of the Christian faith in Igbara-Oke in the late 1800's through the Anglican mission. Father's traditional name was Ifamadesan but as it was done in other parts of Nigeria where the religion was spreading fast, the people embraced the faith and my father, like many others, abandoned traditional worship and took on the name, Gabriel. According to him, he and my mother were later baptized in February, 1913 at the St Paul's Anglican Church, Igbara-Oke, the same church my sister and I were baptised many years later.

Mother died when I was very young so I had no mental picture of what she looked like and it became a bit difficult, more so, as there was no photographs of her that could jog my memory. Nobody in Igbara-Oke had the luxury of owning a camera in those days, therefore, if somebody went away or died, we had nothing to remind us of them. Mother's death was very painful to everyone and no one dared to tell me or my sister how she died. For as long as my maternal grandmother lived, she always betrayed her emotions about my mother's death anytime I visited her. She would burst into tears the minute she saw me and would, thereafter, put me on her laps and begin to weep profusely. I was too young to understand why she always sobbed but as time went by, I began to understand her reason for doing so. The reason, as I later learnt, was because she was unhappy and sad or perhaps pained that mother was not around to see us grow up. Crying whenever she saw us became a sort of routine but after sobbing for few minutes, she would dab her eyes with the tip of her wrapper, signalling the end of the sad emotions she could not control. All the same, no one ever braved it to tell us how our mother died and all those who could, kept closed lips including father. We took consolation only in the fact that many people described her as a very good woman who had ties with Ilesha.

Grandmother Famulayo was from a polygamous home and was the second of her father's children. Her mother (my maternal great-grandmother) was married to a chief in Ijebu-Ere (now called Ere-Ijesha), a village accessible through Ilesa and it was there that she was born. My grandmother had a son at Ijebu-Ere before she moved to Igbara-Oke where she married my grandfather before giving birth to our mother. Grandmother's elder brother was named Patrick Ogunlela but was sometimes called Ogunlala. He grew up and lived in Igbara-Oke also.

My maternal grandmother never spent much time in Igbara-Oke because as a princess of Ijebu-Ere, the tradition forbade her to die outside her place of birth and if she ever did, her corpse must be returned to Ijebu-Ere for burial. Interestingly, and, as if she knew she would die in 1956, she went back to Ijebu-Ere where she died and was buried. Before her death though, she had three daughters; Mama Dorcas was the eldest, followed by my mother, Leah, and the youngest, Rachael. Aunty Rachael later got married to the Obe family – Chief Sapetu. Renowned photographer, Peter Obe, who worked as a photo journalist with *Daily Times*, Barrister Obe and Mike Obe are her three sons.

Papa loved my mother and for many years after her death, he vowed that he was not going to remarry because he was pained by mother's death, so he remained single for many years. However, with two children to take care of, people began to impress it on him to re-marry saying he could not take care of my sister and I all by himself. His reason for not wanting to take another woman according to my father, was because he was so used to our mother and did not want to go through the task of finding another wife. When he eventually decided to re-marry, he tried unsuccessfully to live with seven women over a period of time but he became lucky or fortunate when he tried the eighth time. A woman, Beatrice Ajaja, later called Mama Dupe, was the one who eventually stayed after his many failed attempts.

Mama Dupe was from Igbara-Oke too and she was a very good woman. It took a while for my father to be convinced enough to marry her and but eventually, they got married around 1928 or 1929 and, she would, eventually, outlive my father. Mama Dupe was a very hardworking woman who took my sister and I as her biological children and was very kind to us. For this reason, we loved her and reciprocated her kindness by relating with her as our biological mother. Father loved her a lot, perhaps because she took good care of us. In her account, she said she married our father because of us and because she had always admired the way father treated us, therefore, when father asked her to marry him, she did not hesitate to grant the request.

Growing Up
Apart from farming, father was also into shoe making, a skill he learnt in Ado-Ekiti. He was the only known shoe maker in Igbara-Oke. According to him, he had seen people from Lagos wear different kinds of shoes and

he got interested in knowing how the shoes were made. He made proper shoes, slippers and sandals for sale. When the work was getting too much for him, he employed more hands and though he did not require much help, I still assisted him whenever I had the chance to. I remember that I hated taking drugs in those days and whenever I was sick, he would tell his apprentices to stand by, in case I refused to take the medication. Unlike *agbo* that is cooked, the herbs given to me were never cooked. The leaves were squeezed and drained and the juice extract was given to me to drink. Sometimes the juice was sieved to give a smoother liquid but at other times, we drank it like that, with some leave particles swimming in the liquid. In the course of helping father out and watching him and his apprentices make shoes, I learnt the art and I started making shoes for myself. I had small feet and because of that, I could easily make a good pair of sandals or slippers for myself. After a while, I began making shoes for other people and anytime I was working on any shoe, my father came around to put me through. In some cases, he would give me a salute in appreciation and this always made me happy. His appreciation for what I was doing further encouraged me to try out new designs. He particularly loved calling me *awe* whenever he was impressed with anything I did and this made me very happy.

To survive in those days, you had to do a lot of things to help yourself, therefore, apart from making shoes, I did some barbing also. There were no manual hair clippers, so we used a pair of scissors and locally-made knives. The blades were sharpened with stones before any haircut. Before the advent of matches we used stones on the farm to make fire. There is a part of the palm tree that produces something like wool. We gather some of it and then we take a sharp cutlass to strike a stone, the sparks that come from it goes into the wool and creates a smoke, which we put between dry woods and blow to make fire. Most children also engaged in some profitable ventures like cloth and basket weaving, to make extra money. We cut palm fronds to weave into all sorts of items that could be used for storing cocoa and other farm produce. We were taught cloth weaving in school. The one that men did was taught by people from the north, particularly from Kwara State, because their own loom was different from that of the women. Every student knew something about agriculture and we had agricultural science teachers who supervised us on the school farm. While the boys did the farm work, the girls sold the agricultural products; like cassava, maize, vegetable and so on.

My father was an inspiration to his children and many others. He was very popular in Igbara-Oke and was a chief, just like his father who was the Ojumu of Igbara-Oke. My mother's father too was a chief. He was the Onigemo of Igemo. Father was the Olori-Egbe for his age group in the town, and when he became a Christian, it influenced the decision to make him Olori Egbe in the church also. He was not highly educated, although he wished that he was; nevertheless, he could read the Yoruba Bible very well because for anyone to be baptized in those days, it was a compulsory prerequisite to be able to read the Bible in the native language, master the catechism and believe in the Trinity; God the Father, Jesus Christ the son, and, the Holy Spirit. When Christianity began to expand in Igbara-Oke, the membership was split into two and we had the Olori Egbe 1 and Olori Egbe 2.

My father loved education and having had the privilege of reading the Bible, he seized the opportunity to advance his knowledge and enrolled in evening classes, where he learnt to write. I do not think that he was less than 35 years old when he decided to pursue some formal education.

Armed with the knowledge he gained from reading the Bible and the little education he received from the evening classes, he was able to train himself to read and write. One peculiar thing in those days was that writing was done below the lines instead of writing on the lines and since he was one of the few persons who could read and write, he became the town secretary, a position that he held for a long time. As the secretary, he was expected to write the minutes of every meeting held, and whenever they needed to write a letter to anybody, the onus fell on him to do so. The meetings were always about the progress of Igbara-Oke town.

With his little education, he managed to teach Sarah and I to write, by using any available space on the wall, to teach us numbers and alphabets. We usually painted the walls in the hallway at home with a green leaf so that he could write on it for us. We got our first dose of education by learning figures 1 to 10 and after a while, he taught us how to write 11 to 20. Later on, he taught us the English alphabets. He taught us in Yoruba language and it helped us very much. Since I was his only son, he did not want me out of his sight let alone allow me to go to school. He believed I was still too young to be left alone, which was the same ideology many fathers had in those days. They preferred that we always went to the farm with them.

My Other Siblings

We thank God for the opportunity of making my sister one of the first girls to attend school in Igbara-Oke. Female education was not encouraged at that time because people thought it was a waste of time to send girls to school as they figured that they would not be useful to their family but to another family since, in their opinion, with all their education, they were going to end up in the kitchen. This was a credible argument because at the time, there were no female nurses, no long-term female teachers, and there were no female commissioners! The best of the girls only taught in schools for three years and somebody came to marry them off!

Sister Sarah would, however, stop school in Standard 4, after one of our relatives from Ilorin advised her to come to Ilorin to sit for the entrance examination to gain admission into the School of Nursing. She passed the examination and left for Ilorin at the end of 1938. She too was very protective of me and when she wanted to leave Igbara-Oke, she assured me that she was never going to forget me and would do everything possible to make sure I became successful in life. She was like a mother to me and I depended on her for so many things. She advised me to study hard and promised that if I passed my Standard 6 exams, she would buy lots of things for me. She was happy that I was doing well in school and even prayed to God to take the knowledge in her head and add it to mine, so that I could be great. Such was the love we shared. My older sister is a wonderful woman and it is important to confirm that she lived up to every one of her promises. Fortunately for her, she found Ilorin interesting and she remained there. She was one of the first, if not the very first qualified Nurse from Igbara-Oke. She got married to Mr Joseph Ogbede, who was a manager at U.A.C (Ilorin branch), one of the foremost trading companies in Nigeria at the time, and they are blessed with five wonderful daughters. When I was studying abroad, it was Sister Sarah who took good care of our first son; Jaiye, and our daughter, Kemi, and they see her as their mother.

I later had two brothers and five sisters from the other women that father married but my two brothers died some years later. Nonetheless, I was still close to my other sisters; Mrs. Mary Ebun Elemo, Mrs. Dupe Soleye – the wife of Dr. Onaolapo Soleye of Abeokuta and one-time federal minister, Mrs. Korede Osho, Mrs. Bosede Adebayo – the wife of a house of representative member in Abuja and Mrs. Feyisitan Bodunwa, many of whom were born after I left Igbara-Oke to go and school in Abeokuta.

Memories of My Father

One of my major memories of my father is how much he loved me. Flogging and scolding were not part of my father's training regimen. He was a prayerful man who called for prayers every morning, for all who slept in his house, before anyone went out to the farm or market. Prayers were compulsory, especially for the wives and children. He taught us to always obey adults for our own good and to obey orders and do what is right because that was the only way to avoid trouble. Specifically, he would tell Sarah and I that because we had lost our mother, we should always pick one or two lessons when other children were being rebuked or corrected or advised by their mothers. He reminded us that he would not always be around us forever, therefore, whatever we needed to learn, we should learn without hesitation.

Apart from farming and shoemaking, father also specialized in the treatment of women and children. He rendered the services free and he never took anything in return, though it took a good part of his time, because he always went into the bush to get the herbs he used in making his medications. He was very much loved for his kindness, and for many years, many people depended on him for medications whenever they were sick. Since I did not have interest in native medicine, I did not bother myself so much to know about it. Nevertheless, I am able to identify some herbs that are used for treating some ailments because, sometimes, he sent me to get the herbs for preparing some of the medicines that he used from time to time. Dad was a blessing in his entire life, and was loved by his family, Church and the community. He was about a hundred years old when he died peacefully in 1982. Dad was survived by three wives (Beatrice, Fola and Felie), children, and many grand and great-grand children.

In addition to my other pastime activities, I took interest in playing football. Football was one of the games we enjoyed in those days but I did not get to play it for a long time because my grandmother always got very worried and feared that my legs would be broken, thus, after trying out the game for a while, I gave it up for athletics. My love for athletics grew as a result of my readiness to always go on errands. I would run and dash back in little or no time, and from there, I developed interest in running. If I was not running errands or engaging in house chores, the game of *Ayo* took the centre stage of our activities around the house but whenever we were not doing that, children derived joy in watching the older people play the game. It was played by two people with a wooden case which has six holes on each side. The game was played by putting four *Ayo* seeds in each of the holes and the two players faced each other by moving these seeds while others looked on, sometimes taking sides with any of the two players. After a while of watching adults play the game, the children came up with our own pattern of the game, by digging holes in the ground and playing the game as was done by the elders.

There is a marked difference between the houses we lived in when I was young and modern buildings. In those days, houses were made with clay blocks, and the plastering was done with bare hands. The beds were also made with clay and it was very similar to a slab. All the manpower required to build a house was provided by wives, and perhaps some other members of the family. It was the duty of the women to get the soil while the men moulded the blocks and constructed the building. The clay used during building was usually mixed by kneading it with

the feet to make it stronger. The roofing was made with special wood from the bush. Once the frame of the roof had been constructed, the builders proceeded by using special leaves for covering the building. In the northern part of Nigeria, grasses were used for roofing instead of leaves, but in Igbara-Oke, we used special broad leaves (*ewe gbodogi* and *ewe oguro*). The roofs leaked from time to time when it rained.

Not many people had the privilege of having a room to themselves and I was not exempted, as I had to share the same room with some members of my family. We slept on the mat while father slept on his clay bed. Usually women did not sleep on the bed; they slept on the mats. The main gate to the house was made of wood and it was very fortified. We also had another door at the back of the house leading to the kitchen, which in itself, was a shed at the backyard. Only friends and family members were allowed to go to the back of the house. There were some houses without windows but as people began visiting other places, they began to make windows in their houses. The windows were usually small and were always high up in the building. There was no electricity at that time, so we used mud palm oil lamps and kerosene lanterns. There was no pipe-borne water but we got water from rivers, brooks and from the rain. Letters and messages were sent by hand, from one place to the other, and the bearer travelled on foot, as there were no Post offices, no telephones, no televisions, no buses or taxis. Clocks and watches were rare and thanks to St. Paul's Church, Igbara –Oke, which later had a tall Belfry serving the Church, school, town and the surrounding villages. St. Paul's Church was built with stone and cement walls, roofed with iron rods and covered with special cement sheets.

Life on the Farm
There are two types of palm wine; there is the one you get by

climbing the tree. This is done with the use of what is called *igba*, a sort of rope that is put round the waist of the tapper who uses an axe to cut holes that serve as ladders for the legs, until the tapper gets to the top of the palm tree where the wine supply is. The other palm tree is the one that has branches already. In this case the branches are cut off and the tapper goes from one tree to another, collecting the juice. We call that *oguro*. *Emu* is the wine made from the palm trees that are found anywhere but *oguro* is from the palm trees by the river side. Usually, I felled the palm trees by the road side by cutting it, either by the root, or from the stem, and when it was felled, we took our supply. I climbed the trees a few times to see how it felt up there or to get a supply. The palm wine was for drinking and also, for sale. It was used at ceremonies and sometimes for relaxation on the farm.

Yam was a yearly produce. You plant, and after some months, you harvest, as with other crops, but cocoa takes a longer process. It could take four or five years for it to produce fruit but once it begins to yield, the benefits are reaped for years. Cocoa is a long-term investment that does not allow any other tree to be planted beside it because after a while, it creates shades that would not allow other plants to grow. There were times when the work required that we hired labourers during the harvest to assist us. For most people, they planted crops for consumption only, and it is when they have excess that they sell, but as a good family man, men made sure that their family was well-fed before they considered selling their farm harvests.

Life in the village was peaceful and exciting, but, by the 1930s, things had begun to change gradually. Many Nigerians were getting educated and were beginning to leave the village for the cities, in search of education, and a better life that farming could neither provide nor sustain. As it

would please God, He made a divine arrangement for me to be part of this group!

Chief Gabriel Ojo – my father

Chief Mrs Sarah Omowunmi Ogbede – my sister

CHAPTER TWO

PASSPORT TO KNOWLEDGE

"Thus says the Lord who made you and formed you from the womb, **who** *will help you: 'Fear not."*
- **Isaiah 44:2b**

Although I was born in 1923, I did not start school until 1934, being an only son. Besides, father loved me so much that he never for a moment wanted me out of his sight. He loved my sister too and he gave her all the freedom she needed and allowed her to go to school but insisted that I had to stay with him. In those days, farmers usually carried big bags where they kept their cutlasses and hoes while the children and the wives carried the farm produce and firewood. The women and children would walk ahead while the men came behind as they made their way home from the farm.

My journey to school began one sunny evening in March 1934 when my father and I were on our way home from the farm. That afternoon, I came across the man who would hand over to me, the passport that would turn my life around forever. St. Paul's Primary school was the only primary school in Igbara-Oke in those days and the headmaster, Archdeacon S.O. Akinluyi was a very disciplined and well-read man. He loved education so much that he always frowned at parents who did not enrol their children in school. To get to the church from the road, one had to ascend 32 steps, and every evening, Archdeacon Akinluyi was always either descending or ascending those steps. Everybody in Igbara-Oke found his action very amusing. It was father who explained to me later, that it was one of the ways the Archdeacon communed with God!

On that fateful day, and as though he was waiting for father and I to walk by, the Archdeacon stopped us in our tracks and beckoned on father, saying that he wanted to speak with him. The discussion centred on my education and Archdeacon Akinluyi gave father so many convincing reasons why he should send me to school instead of trying to make a farmer of me. He told father that some of my age mates were in school already and it would be wrong for him to prevent me from being educated like them.

After his 'sermon', father tried to defend his hold on me by telling the Archdeacon that I was not ripe for school yet. Ignorantly, father added that it was not going to be possible for me to be in school at that time of the year because it was April and school was in session already, but the Archdeacon was not bought over by father's line of argument. Stoically, he educated father on how the school calendar ran, saying, that it was time I went off to school. From where I was standing, it appeared that the Archdeacon had won the battle because father had no response, and from his mien, it was all too certain that my progression to the gates of the school, and eventually, the classroom, was soon to be fired in motion. The Archdeacon closed his argument when he announced that without delay, he was ready to admit me into St. Paul's Primary School. Father could not object any further and he consented to the advice of the Archdeacon. On our arrival home that day, I shared the news with everybody. It was a happy moment for me.

St. Paul's Primary School, Igbara-Oke (1934-1940)

I started school on April 10, 1934, a few weeks after the encounter with Archdeacon Akinluyi. Since I could read and write appreciably to some extent, I began my primary education from Primary One. Full primary school in those days was for eight years: two years in the infant department and the remaining six at the primary level. We were 12 pupils in my class – Olagbaiye, Ladi Obe, Thomas Apata, Odesola, Bisi Adedeji, Eunice Odeyemi, who became the wife of the late King of Igbara-Oke and, Felicia Monisade, who became Mrs. Obe, were some of my classmates. Out of the 12 of us, Eunice and Felicia were the only girls. St. Paul's School was the only full primary school around at that time, which was the reason pupils from neighbouring areas like Ogotun, Ilawe, Aramoko and Akure came to study for their Standards Four to Six certificate examinations in the school, in order to obtain their first school leaving certificates, as the last two classes were not available in other towns. This made Igbara-Oke very popular.

Of the 12 pupils in my class who sat for the Standard Six examinations in 1940, all 12 of us passed. Of these persons, I remember Chief Olagbaiye, Mr. Ladi Obe, who lived in the house next to our church. There was also Thomas Apata and Odesola, who lived close to the Adedeji family, both of whom are late.

To be admitted into primary school in those days, you were made to put one of your arms across your head and you only qualified if your fingers covered your ears. The process was done to know whether a child was old enough for school, as many parents did not know the ages of their children. My father wrote down my date of birth when I was born, therefore, I did not do the test. All that was required were my names, age and the names of my parents. Once that information was supplied, you were assured of a place in school. I resumed school the day I was enrolled because the registration was not so tasking. Sister Sarah took me to school that first day and I found the environment exciting as most of the pupils were children I was familiar with. Our school uniform was brown khaki shorts and shirt, but the shirt was later changed to a mesh of green and yellow.

A typical school day began with the sound of the bell signalling that it was time for morning assembly. If you were on your way to school and you heard the bell, you were expected to run as fast as you could to beat the eight o'clock resumption time as failure to beat it always attracted punishment. At exactly eight o'clock, we all filed to the assembly, in separate rows of boys and girls. After we assembled, the presiding teacher would read a passage from the Bible to us, and afterwards, give lessons on how to be good boys and girls. I remember one story in particular told by a teacher of a shepherd boy who always cried wolf when there was none. The boy cried wolf on two occasions and many people ran to help him and his sheep, only to get there and see that the boy was just joking. On the third occasion when he cried "wolf, wolf", nobody hearkened to his call for help. Unfortunately, it was on that third occasion, that a wolf indeed appeared and it devoured all his sheep.

We were trained to tell the truth always, at all times and to be careful of the things we said. After we are admonished to live a good life, inspections would then be carried out by the teachers. Many pupils feared this moment because they often ran afoul of sanitary rules. During inspection, the teachers looked at our finger nails, bodies and uniforms, to check

whether they were unclean or torn. After the inspection, prayers would follow and then announcements would be made before we marched to our different classrooms with the school band playing – drums, flute and singing. I played the flute in the school band. We had a period for games and sports between classes. Often times, announcements were made to inform us of a football match between our school and any neighbouring school or about any new development in the school.

One thing every pupil dreaded in those days was chastisement. Punishment was severe and it was an unofficial part of the school curriculum. Only the headmaster and the trained teachers were allowed to use the whip, while all the junior teachers could only engage pupils in manual labour after school hours, which usually came in form of cutting grass and, a reprimand we all detested because of the pain we had to endure. I was quite a good boy but one day I was unduly whipped by a teacher who accused me falsely of making jest of a girl in class. He did not allow me to explain what I was really laughing at, which had nothing to do with the girl. In real fact, the teacher was involved in an illicit affair with a female student. You could be flogged on your palm but if the teachers wanted to be wicked, you could be flogged below your bottom. That was where I was flogged. I was never troublesome. I was disciplined from home and my father would not condone any indiscipline or truancy. In any case, I did not have any reason to play truancy.

I managed to get home but the next day, when I could not get up, my grandmother was very angry and wanted to make a case out of it but people prevailed on her not to, because I could be punished again. That incident was one of my low-points in the primary school while one of the high-points for me was the Empire Day celebrations.

Some teachers made a good impression on me. In the primary school, two teachers in particular; Chief Komolafe and Mr. B.A. Falana, inspired me. Chief Komolafe made a lasting impression on me. He was the first person to take a collective photograph of his class in Standard Five. He would later come to see me in the hospital in 1982 when I was not feeling well. He brought the picture he took in 1939 and said, "Look at the picture that we took then". I still have that picture. That was the first picture I ever saw myself in. The other teacher, Mr. B.A. Falana was the infant master and it was he who later helped me to get admission into Baptist Boys High School (B.B.H.S) in Abeokuta because he was a native of Abeokuta.

The Empire Day was an annual event held on May 24, all over Nigeria, to celebrate the monarchy in England and we sang the British anthem – *God save the King,* but that changed on October 1, 1960, after Nigeria gained her independence that brought an end to the colonial rule. Empire Day was marked in different regions with so many events, especially sporting activities. For Igbara-Oke and its environs, the event took place annually in Akure, Ondo Province and pupils from other schools came together to compete in the sporting events. The journey to Akure was always memorable. We travelled in a lorry and the school also provided us with food, which was what many of us constantly looked forward to, apart from the fact that we wanted to make new friends. As one of the best athletes, I was well known around Ondo and I learnt so much from being an athlete. I learnt that cooperation was good in everything one did and that endurance and focus were some of the skills that are needed to become the first in anything I did. It paid off for me because in the 100-yard race in 1939, I came first and the prize was a school uniform for the following year. I also came first in 440-yard race in 1939 and second place in 1940.

Apart from my passion for running, I was a very active member of the Boys' Brigade and a member of the church school choir. I played the flute, which gave me a good avenue to develop my talent as a treble singer. Another high point when I was in primary school was the closing day exercise when parents were invited to school to watch their children perform and assess them in extra-curricular and academic activities. We recited songs and poems in Yoruba and English, acted dramas and performed other entertainment activities and I took an active part in many of them.

English language and Bible knowledge were two of my best subjects and being one of the best pupils in class with one of the best handwritings, I was made the editor of the school magazine, *naturally*. It was fun and a great privilege for me because whenever other pupils were engaged in manual labour, I worked on the magazine. I collected write-ups from my mates and re-wrote them before finally putting them on the notice board. Apart from editing the magazine, I also learnt cloth weaving and carpentry during free periods.

Sensing that I could not rely solely on my father for all the things I needed in the primary school, I sold kerosene and matches in the evenings around the town and fire wood to food sellers at *Obada* Market in the day time, to help myself financially. I saved part of the money I made from those sales and from it, I bought some of the things I needed in school, including paying for sewing my choir robe and getting two outfits while my father paid my school fees and bought the things I could not afford. Other kids in Igbara-Oke also hawked to support their parents. I had a hawking partner, named Rufus Aiyegbo. We hawked and played together but he was financially better-off than I was because he also sewed army uniforms and made sure he supported me whenever I needed help. Despite the fact that I was engaged in trading, I made sure that I studied conscientiously throughout my stay in the primary school.

I sat for my First School Leaving Certificate examination in 1940, the result came out a year after, and although all 12 of us in my class passed, three of us did exceptionally well and were given automatic employment as pupil teachers in the primary schools around Igbara-Oke, in 1941. As pupil teachers, we were allowed to teach pupils in Standards 1 to 3 but could not teach the upper grades because we were not trained teachers and we lacked the necessary experience. The higher classes were handled by Grade II certified teachers who had graduated from teacher-training colleges such as St. Andrews College, Oyo or the Baptist College, Iwo.

I was posted to Ogotun. Lorries did not go there often but there was a bush path you could take. Ogotun had adjacent bush paths. Taking the paths made the journey half. When I went to Ogotun, my stepmother assisted me to carry some of my belongings through that path. I was in Ogotun for two years. The school manager in Igbara-Oke was the one who supervised all the schools in the area. He was also responsible for paying salaries. His name is Bishop I.O.S. Okusanya and was formerly a Reverend. He was from Ijebu. He was a very strong man and he was highly educated. He was one of the first Nigerians to study at Fourah-Bay College in Sierra Leone because there was no university in Nigeria then. Unless God opened the gates of England for you, you could not go anywhere else except Fourah Bay College. Bishop Okusanya was one of the first few people to get formal education in Nigeria.

After it was impressed on father to allow me to go to school on the admonition of the Bishop and headmaster of the primary school in Igbara-Oke, he tried all he could to pay my school fees but it got a little difficult for him at a time. Any time we did not pay, we would be sent home and the only option was to go to the farm, which some of us had come to detest after we started school. To avoid going to the farm, we had to seek other ways of being productive and other avenues to make money. This led me into selling firewood at one point because I needed money to buy pencils, books and some other school items. In those days, there was a limit to which I could demand money from father and knowing that we did not have a mother and could not run to any other person, and even if we did, some of them would have told us to go and look at some of our mates, to see what they do hence, I had to do all I could to make money. A basket of firewood could sell for a penny and one could use half a penny for breakfast and still keep some part of the money. The value of money at that time was very okay and I abhorred the temptation of running away with any of the lorries that brought firewood to Igbara-Oke.

The financial hardship I faced became almost unbearable when father was swindled by money doublers. It was a serious thing. Father's main income was from selling palm wine. The tricksters invaded Igbara-Oke and they targeted some people whom they felt had money. They thought my father was rich because he was one of the three people who owned a bicycle in the town. My father's bicycle was the strongest because it was a Hercules. The other victims had Raleigh and one of them was a trader at Odo-Oja. He was from Ilesa and had three sons. The third person was a woman who sold food at Obada. Our bicycles were well known around because we rode from one end of the town to another and we could do some acrobatic displays on them. The tricksters convinced my father that they could help him make more money. They requested for 20 pounds promising to double it by performing some tricks and he did as was demanded. The tricksters then wrapped something in a cloth and asked him and his fellow victims to put it in an enclosed place in their rooms. They were directed to open the wrapped clothes after seven days. What they found inside was surprising. The tricksters cut paper into the size of money and put real money on top in order to deceive their victims. Interestingly, they gave their victims the same day to open their expected wealth. Prior to the D-day, the dupes went to town making merry and drinking palm wine, pretending that they were genuine, only to disappear on the eve of the D-day. When father brought out his own package, he was heart-broken by what he discovered. Like him, the other victims discovered a fast one had been pulled on them. The three policemen in Igbara-Oke at the time were not trained to curb such excesses, and they could not arrest the tricksters.

It affected our family so much and for a long time we all suffered the loss but my stepmother and father sacrificed a lot to cushion the effect. One morning, after the incident, before father and his wife set out to go to the farm, they woke us up and told us there was yam for us in the pot, because for a long time, we found it very hard to eat at home. They also left some money for us in case we needed to buy anything. We were surprised and wondered where they got money from but our curiosity lapsed when we learnt that father had sold the bicycle so he could have money to take care of us. It was a bad year for us but father got over the incident with the aid of the sale of some produce from his farm. I was able to continue with my education after the setback and with God's help, I was able to complete my primary education in Igbara-Oke.

I taught in Ogotun for two years, after which I returned to Igbara-Oke in 1943 to teach at St. Paul's Primary School for a year. Technological advancement was minimal and there was no electricity, houses made from cement blocks, computer or jobs in those days. The common job you could get in the 1930's and 1940's was teaching; if you were fortunate enough to get a job, and the salary was not so buoyant. Rev I O S Okusanya was the School Manager. He was a respected father and leader. He taught us in the Boys Brigade to work with our hands and save our few shillings and pennies for our future need. Yet there were no Banks or Post Office offices around to safely keep money. When I luckily became a Pupil teacher under him, 1941-1943, I saved with him ten shillings per month for three years (eighteen pounds) out of my total salary. When I started teaching in 1941 at Ogotun, I earned 15 shillings, six pence monthly. The second year it was 17 shillings and six pence and the third year, it became one pound, monthly. Although it was an appreciable sum of money, I was not satisfied because I wanted to develop myself more. This handsome saving of eighteen pounds was all I had and depended upon to start my secondary school education. I was one of five classmates of twelve to have the unique opportunity of secondary school education.

A Grade II teacher in St. Paul's, Mr. B.A. Falana, saw my yearning for education and advised me to seek admission in a secondary school. Bishop I.O.S. Okusanya, the school manager also supported the idea. In those days, there were only four government-owned secondary schools in the Western region: Anglican Grammar School, Ilesa; Ondo Boys High School, Ondo; Ijebu-Ode Grammar School, Ijebu-Ode and Abeokuta Grammar School, Abeokuta. They were called the I.O.I.A. Schools after their locations. All four did their inter-house sports at the same time and played inter-school football matches. In the West, the Anglican, Methodist and Baptist churches had secondary schools in Ibadan, Ondo, Ijebu-Ode, Ilesha, Abeokuta and Ado-Ekiti, and Teacher's Colleges in Iwo, Ibadan and Oyo. The government schools were doing quite well but they were not as organized or adequately funded as the mission schools, therefore, Mr. B.A. Falana suggested that I go to the mission school but, I was rejected at St Andrews College, Oyo for the simple reason that my father was a polygamist!

Baptist Boys High School, Abeokuta (1944-1946)

With the help of Mr. Falana, I applied to Baptist Boys High School (B.B.H.S)[1] Abeokuta which, compared to other schools, was inexpensive and had an edge because of the input of foreign missionary tutors. I took the entrance examination in 1943, passed, and was given admission in 1944. I was so elated. Another chapter of my life was about to begin. Preparations for Abeokuta began in earnest. I managed to get a few things but there was still a big challenge. I did not have enough money to take to Abeokuta apart from the eighteen pounds I had saved as a pupil teacher. My father did not have enough money; besides, he was sick and needed help himself. There was no one to run to, nevertheless, I was bent on going to B.B.H.S. When it was time to leave for school, my father gave me his blessings and I left Igbara-Oke for Abeokuta in 1944, with faith and hope that things would turn out for the better. Whilst still at the B.B.H.S., my stepmother handed over my sister, Dupe, to take with me and train her. Since there was no one to defray the huge expenses of being in the school hostel, I decided to be a day student. By God's divine providence, I met Rev. and Mrs. Odeneye who gave my sister Dupe and I accommodation in their home, which, fortunately for me, was very close to the school. I worked hard on my studies, I took lessons on typing after school hours. The town itself looked very different from Igbara-Oke

---

[1] https://en.wikipedia.org/wiki/Baptist_Boys%27_High_School

and the people were more enlightened because of the close affinity and, perhaps, proximity they had with Lagos.

In the whole of Abeokuta, B.B.H.S. had some of the best structures (buildings) and you could feel an aura of seriousness exude from everywhere the moment you entered the school. The structures were well-kempt while the flowers and grass were pruned and primed constantly. Orderliness was second nature around B.B.H.S. and it transcended the premises of the school. The first day I set my feet on the school premises, I was glad that I chose B.B.H.S. Around the school, discipline was second nature also, and the teachers were highly trained and meticulous in the discharge of their duties. Considering the fact that it was a mission school, morals and values, as expected, were an unwritten code and, above everything, Godliness was very important if you wanted to be successful in the school.

I was admitted into Class Two in B.B.H.S. because of my brilliant performance at the entrance examination. Just like I experienced in the primary school, I learnt quickly in Abeokuta, that attendance at the school assembly and in class was not to be toyed with. We resumed classes immediately after the morning assembly and teachers were very prompt in class because the school authority did not joke with academics. Even with my financial incapacity, I still managed to do well in my studies. In my third year, when my sister, Sarah got a job as a qualified nurse, she began sending me pocket money occasionally, and that solved part of my financial problems. Nevertheless, I continued hoping for things to get better.

The School motto was *Nulli Secundus* which means "Second to none." A favourite text and challenge to students by the teachers was "You are our epistle written in our hearts, known and read by all men (2 Corinthians 3:2)."

Saved by Grace, Not by Works

My understanding of a good Christian was different. I felt that since I was singing in the school choir and serving the school in various capacities, I was worthy of being called a Christian but that notion changed in 1946 when a Rev. J.A. Ajani came to B.B.H.S. to hold a revival for staff and students of the school. In his sermon, Rev. Ajani told us that salvation was a personal thing, as good works alone could not guarantee the salvation of our souls or a place in heaven, adding that Christianity required surrendering one's life to God. He went on to quote a passage in the Bible that says, "all our righteousness is like filthy rags before God (Isaiah 64:6)" and that it was by accepting Jesus Christ as our Lord and Saviour that we could be saved.

I was touched by the message. It shot chilly fervours down my body. After a deep thought, I acknowledged that I lacked the Holy Spirit and the only way to have Him was by giving my life to Jesus Christ. After the sermon, I knew that it was time to accept Christ since salvation was not by works but by grace. Without further delay, I accepted Jesus Christ as my Lord and Saviour and shortly after, I got baptized at Ago-Owu Baptist Church by Dr. J.T. Ayorinde. I had been baptized by sprinkling as an infant and confirmed in the Anglican Church but this time, baptism was by immersion, the Baptist way, which to me, is the Bible way. I faced no challenges after I became born again because I had given the rightful place to Jesus Christ in my life. Now I had to live as He – God, wanted me to live. In my opinion, I had always been a good person because of my love for Jesus and I felt I had to continue but now I had to think of others, their salvation and well-being and so on. I learnt to begin to live a useful

life. My father was very happy about my decision. He did not raise any objection but it was later when I went into the Baptist ministry that he wished I had stayed an Anglican and became an Anglican reverend but he was not against my decision.

Although I was doing well in school, much to my displeasure, I could not cope with the financial demands of my education any more, therefore I quit school to look for a job. I read my books at night, using the street lights for illumination. My only consolation was to keep on putting my trust in God and He did not fail me. A glimmer of hope came a few weeks later when I was told about a very wealthy school proprietor in Ijebu-Ode (Chief Adeola Odutola, popularly known as Ogbeni Oja) who could allow me to finish my secondary education, freely, in his school – Adeola Odutola College. I wrote to him as advised, requesting for assistance to get through classes five and six and offering to serve as one of his workers. When I waited anxiously and did not get a reply, I decided to go to Ijebu-Ode to see him. With the approval of the Odeneye's, I left for Ijebu-Ode in a lorry, hoping and praying in my heart to meet the man and more critically, that he would grant my request. I got safely to the man's place only to be told that he was away for the weekend and would not be back until late on Sunday. I was disillusioned but I resolved that since I had made the long journey to Ijebu-Ode, there was no point leaving just like that. Another voice, however, kept telling me to leave since I would not have a place to pass the night but the former prevailed and I decided to stay.

Fortunately for me, I met one of the rich man's workers and explained my mission to Ijebu-Ode to him. He sympathized with my plight and since I could not go back to Abeokuta that night, he offered to allow me to stay with him in the boys' quarters till Sunday when his boss would return. The man was very kind to me. Apart from providing where to stay, he also gave me food but I was anxious to meet Chief Odutola and my anxiety grew throughout that weekend. It was as if Chief Odutola was taking forever to come back. When he did return on Sunday night as expected, his worker who sheltered me said it was impossible for me to see him that evening since he just returned from a trip; moreover, he did not know me. I agreed with him, although not utterly.

On Monday morning, I woke up early and prepared to meet Chief Odutola on whom, I believed, my destiny depended so much upon. I got to his office by 8:30 a.m. but did not see him until 11:00 a.m. While I waited near his office, he was going in and out and dishing out orders to his numerous workers to get some things for his children who were going back to school that day. When I finally saw him and explained my mission, I was taken aback by his response. He said it was impossible to allow me to come and finish my education in his school. That was it, he did not say more. I tried to plead with him to give me a chance, but everything I said to make him appreciate what finishing my education meant to me, made no impact on him. Not believing what I had just heard, I walked out of his office with a feeling of dejection and with my heart crippled by sadness. It was unbelievable to me that someone who, before our meeting, was asking his workers to get all sorts of things for his children, could be so insensitive to my own plight. That vision kept on playing in my mind and I wished I could erase it but I could not. I resigned to fate and headed to the boys' quarters to get my things. I told the man who accommodated me what happened and he consoled and wished me well, before I finally took my exit from the school and headed for the motor park.

As I headed to the motor park, despair built up in my soul. I kept on wondering what I was going to do next. By the time I got to the motor park, the lorries going to Abeokuta from Ijebu-Ode were all gone. There were no travellers in sight and I did not want to sleep in the boys' quarters again. I then began wandering about, looking for where to pass the night until I came across a band of town hunters who were on patrol. They asked what I was looking for around Ijebu-Ode at that time of the night. I begged them and told them my predicament. Convinced by my story, they took me in and allowed me to stay with them till the next morning, but I could not sleep. I was too devastated by the outcome of my unrealized mission and I was scared of the armed hunters too. At the first crow of the cock the following morning, the hunters led me to the motor park and I left with the first lorry going to Abeokuta on that day.

When I returned to Abeokuta and told the Odeneye's the outcome of my trip to Ijebu-Ode, they were not happy but Mama Odeneye was very hopeful and advised me to not allow the problem to weigh me down as the Lord would take control of the situation. I could not go to school again because the principal had written to my father about my school fees but my father was helpless. There was nothing he could do. Sister Sarah tried the best she could to help me, but her efforts were not enough to keep me in school. Although I had to stay away from school, it was only for a short period because God proved to me again, that He was with me.

Lifeline

Early in 1947, I was given a lifeline to go back to B.B.H.S. but, this time, as a librarian and not a student. The school previously employed librarians on a part-time basis but on this occasion, they needed someone on a permanent basis who could man the library from morning till evening. I applied for the job and I was employed immediately as the first permanent school librarian in B.B.H.S. It did not matter much to me if I was returning to B.B.H.S. as a librarian and not a student, all I had on my mind was that I needed money urgently and if I had to earn it, I just must take any job that came my way.

As a librarian at B.B.H S., my duty was to open the library at 3.00 a.m. because real studies began around 8:30 a.m. after the morning devotion. I attended to both staff and students which made me very popular around the school. Not long after I was employed, library periods were incorporated into the school time-table. This allowed the different classes to visit the library at the specified periods. It was fun doing the job because I always came across some of my classmates in the library. I did not feel ashamed seeing them; rather, I was happy because I knew what I was doing and I had set a goal for myself. Though the job was a little tasking, I was able to cope with all the demands through God's help. My work as a librarian was to sort and arrange the books back on the shelf after they are read. I also took inventory of every new material coming into the library while also making sure everything was in order.

My forced decision to abandon school did not, however, deter me from marching on in life as I managed to finish my secondary education through my resolve to write the Cambridge School Certificate Examination as an external candidate. I knew that if I did that and I passed, I could come down to Lagos, get a better and well-paying job that would take care of my needs. The good thing about the job was that it gave me the opportunity to prepare for my Cambridge external examinations which many people did not know about, and by God's grace, everything worked out as planned.

While my mates were in class, I would seize that opportunity to study on my own, discreetly. Whenever my friends came to the library, I would ask for their note books and copy what they were taught in class. I did

that until I registered as a private student for the Cambridge School Certificate Examination in Abeokuta; thanks to the money I was able to save from working as a librarian. I could not write the exam in B.B.H.S. as that would mean doing so ahead of my classmates but I wrote the examination later in 1947 and, with God's help and hard work, I passed excellently. When the result was released, I came out with Grade II while my classmates in B.B.H.S. were just passing to their final year. I had a pass in English but if I had gotten a credit in English language like the other subjects, it would have meant being exempted from sitting for the London matriculation examination. So I had to take the English language examination again the same year and when the result came out, I passed excellently.

Baptist Boys High School, Abeokuta

With my Cambridge School Certificate result and London matriculation examination exemption status, I could be admitted into any university in any British colony but I chose otherwise, and decided to move to Lagos to seek further avenues to improve my life. Moreover, what I was earning was not going to be enough to take care of my needs and that of the family if I decided to continue working as a librarian. When I told the Odeneyes of my plan, they were very pleased that I was finally able to get something from my secondary education after all the initial setbacks. Secondly, they were also overjoyed that I could now get a better job to help myself. I had a wonderful time staying with them because throughout my stay, they acted like my surrogate parents and they did the best they could to make life comfortable for me.

In the middle of 1948, I left Abeokuta for Lagos to stay with my friend Abiodun Aloba whom I called Biodun. Abiodun Aloba, also known as Ebenezer Williams, was a staff of UAC. He was of Benin origin but lived with his family in Igbara-Oke and we had been good friends from childhood. He was the one who invited me to Lagos for the very first time when I visited the city in 1946. On that first visit, I saw Lagos as a wonderful place because, compared to Igbara-Oke and Abeokuta, it was more developed, with a number of physical structures and infrastructure. Biodun had his own apartment in Lagos and was living pretty comfortably since he had a good job. My first visit was quite an experience because I helped Biodun to sell some copies of the book he wrote about Nnamdi Azikiwe. The book was called "ZIK as I know him". Biodun was a journalist and a strong believer in, and supporter, of the ideologies of Nigeria's first President, Dr. Nnamdi Azikwe. He was a staunch admirer of the man and his love for him propelled him to write the book in his honour. Since I had nothing to do, I just took some copies of the book when he was off to work and went out to sell them. I began by selling the books around his place in Surulere, and later, in Ebute-Metta and its environs.

On the first day, I was able to sell quite a number of copies considering that I had garnered enough experience from hawking back in Igbara-Oke. When Biodun returned from work that day and I gave him the proceeds from the books sold, he was very surprised and happy. I did the same thing for the rest of my stay in Lagos and he kindly rewarded my effort. When I was going back to Abeokuta he gave me some money which was a good relief for me because of the strained financial status I was in at that period. Before I left though, I visited some places in Lagos like Obun-Eko and Ina-Bere. Many people from Igbara-Oke that I knew were staying in Ina-Bere and I visited them once in a while before I left for Abeokuta. That first visit opened my eyes to so many things as well as the opportunities in Lagos and I concluded in my mind that after that first visit, I would come back to Lagos to get a good job.

Having passed my Cambridge School Certificate Examination with an exemption from writing the London Matriculation, I resigned my job as a librarian in B.B.H.S. Before I left Abeokuta, I told one of my teachers in B.B.H.S. that I wanted to move to Lagos so that I could get a good job and start a new life and he promised to assist me through his fiancée. His girlfriend was working at the Labour office in Lagos and he sent a message to her that somebody would be coming to Lagos, whom she needed to assist in getting a job. The lady obliged and she helped me to get a labour card (ID/work permit) that assisted me in getting a job at the Electricity Corporation, Lagos.

Leaving Abeokuta was emotive for me. It was as if I was leaving a part of me behind because of the many people who had made a great impact in my life. I remember with gratitude to God, the spiritual and physical blessings I received from Dr. and Mrs. I. N. Patterson, Rev. and Mrs. B. T. Griffin, Dr. E.L. Akinsanya, Rev. S.A. Lawoyin, Dr. E. A. Dahunsi, Dr. F. A. Awobodu, B.O. Ojoomu and Mr. Johnson. These people showed me kindness and love. The spiritual blessings I received from them were enormous because they lived an exemplary life as Christians. They proved that they were true Christians by the way they lived their lives. They were honest in their works and were untiring in their service to God. When I was in B.B.H.S., they constantly reminded me that like epistles, B.B.H.S. would be a reference point wherever I went to. They taught us to be thorough in whatever we did and to say the truth at all times. We were taught to live right and act like an epistle that would be read by everyone; Christians and non-Christians, old or young.

I am eternally grateful to the Principals and staff of B.B.H.S. for the good foundation given to us in the school. I left the school with happy memories. Rev. and Mrs. Odeneye not only allowed us to live in their home but provided Godly and timely counsel for which I equally grateful. My classmates included Mr. Makinde from Igbara-Oke, Aaron Akinbola, Bantefa, Alhaji Adesanya and Professor Anthonio. Professor Adeoye Adeniyi was a school mate.

Life in Lagos
I left Abeokuta finally in the middle of 1948 for Lagos. I resumed immediately at Electricity Corporation of Nigeria (E.C.N.) and I was posted to the meter room. My duty was to check the light meters to determine whether they were regulated properly or not, before they were distributed to consumers. I did that for a while until I got tired of the job, partly because of a bitter experience I had at the company. The

woman who sold food to us was very nice and accommodating, initially, until one day when she embarrassed me by demanding that I paid before I ate the food she had served me already. The practice before then was that we could buy food on credit and pay at a later date but on that day, she snapped and said she wanted her money. I did not have enough money with me and it was a big embarrassment to me because she asked one of her service girls to take the food away from me. The other reason I got fed up with the job was because my salary could not take care of my transportation expenses. I was living across the railway crossing in Surulere and it was a long way from E.C.N. which was on Broad Street on the Lagos Island (over 5 miles/8 kilometres). I remembered a particular day that I walked from Ina- Bere in Ebute-Meta to my place in Surulere as I did not have enough money with me. I was very sorry for myself that day, thus, the poor proximity to the office from my home and the humiliation I received from the food seller at E.C.N. were the two reasons for which I quit my job.

Not long after I made up my mind to quit, I heard that there were openings in the Chief Mechanical Engineer's office at the Nigerian Railway Corporation in Ebute-Meta close to where I live. I applied, and immediately two of us were given employment. This time round, the job at the Nigerian Railways was quite challenging and the conditions of service were very fair. Nobody in Igbara-Oke, except my sister, knew my whereabouts then but after a while, I got in touch with some relatives at home to inform them that I was now working in Lagos and was staying with Biodun. They were happy because he was somebody they knew and liked so well. Biodun would in later years, become my brother-in-law.

The Nigeria Railway was a very good place to work in, in those days. The job allowed you to be exposed to so many good experiences and

I benefited a lot from working there. I did not want to rely only on my salary, so I engaged in selling Christian magazines after closing hours and Christmas cards whenever the yuletide was approaching. I did that so that I could earn some extra income. I was earning 96 pounds per annum, which was handsome money at that time. The lessons I learnt in my younger days in Igbara-Oke, about trading, helped me again because I knew how to get my supplies to Nigeria, from abroad. The cards and magazines were produced by different overseas firms and I was ordering the merchandise directly from London. When I was going to get married in 1955, my knowledge of importing items from abroad became useful and aided me in purchasing our wedding rings from London. I later began ordering different items, on demand, for my friends who wanted to get married.

Learning to Say 'No': My Big Bicycle Bruise

> "My son, if sinners entice thee, consent thou not."
> - Proverbs 1: 10 KJV

I cannot forget the day I had a bitter experience with my bicycle in Lagos, all in a bid to make a good impression. A friend of mine who was working at the Nigeria Airways in Lagos invited me to her birthday party. Both our sisters were good friends at the nursing school in Ilorin. We usually met there whenever we visited our sisters during the holidays. We became good friends and I cannot remember what year but she invited me to her birthday party in Lagos. Days before the party, I took out my best pair of trousers, ironed it and looked forward to the party. When the day finally came, I woke up early and began counting down the hours because my mind was already at the place. When it was 2 O'clock in the afternoon, I dressed in my well-ironed clothes and after looking in the mirror, I did not need anyone to tell me how debonair I looked. I mounted my Rudge bicycle and sped along the way from my house in Surulere to the venue in Ebute-Meta, whizzing past houses and people, feeling an unusual burst of joy. My bicycle was always the cynosure of all eyes because of the special accessories that came with it. When I arrived at the party, I met some boys and girls there. My hostess was very happy to see me and thereafter I was ushered to a seat.

After settling down, I began to peer at the few guests who had arrived so that I could get acquainted with some of the faces. More guests began to saunter in while I sat alone, with my mind drifting every minute to my best pair of trousers. Minutes later, a lady came to serve us some bottles of Stout, which I had never taken before. Apart from palm wine, I had never taken any other form of alcohol, so I felt there was no harm in having a taste of the drink for the first time. I requested for a bottle, had it opened and for minutes, I kept on wondering what was inside it because the bottle was particularly dark on the outside. Seconds after, I decided to brave it by taking one little sip from the bottle. The content was cold and a bitter chill enveloped my mouth. I did not, however, want to betray my emotions because when I looked around, other boys were drinking and they seemed to be enjoying themselves. Wanting to feel bold, I took another large gulp from the bottle and felt another bitter chill in my mouth, but this time, it was a subdued one. Moments later, I observed that I was not feeling the way I felt prior to taking the drink. My vision was getting blurred by the minute and I began to feel tipsy. Immediately I was sure my vision was becoming impaired, I took a hurried exit out of the venue, but not before I had told my host that I was leaving. All her pleas that I stayed back did not mean much because I was beginning to feel uncomfortable.

While I meandered to where my bicycle was parked, I felt my legs wobble but I managed to mount on my prized two-wheeled object and set out on the journey home. While on the bicycle, I could feel a flurry of unusual zest in me and about a few kilometres to the Ebute-Meta post office, I slammed myself to the ground. My bicycle had hit something and I lay sprawled on the ground. I was on the floor for minutes writhing in pain and when I managed to regain a bit of consciousness, I felt a pain on my knee cap. It was bruised and, immediately I felt the pain surge from my knee, my mind wafted to my favourite pair of trousers which by this time was torn at the knee. After examining the tear and I managed to get up, I saw a few eyes focused on me. I was not sure if they were sympathizing with me or they were just uncaring about my predicament. I dusted my torn pair of trousers, picked up my bicycle which I had ignored to tend to my best pair of trousers, raised it and managed to mount on it again. Ignoring the many eyes that were still glued on me, I rode away from the spot feeling downcast and sorry for myself. I decided that day that I would never touch alcohol. Thinking through the event, I found me asking myself; "Why didn't you just take a stand and refuse the offer?" Through that experience, I learnt that in every situation, we always have a choice to say 'no' and it is more honourable to say 'no' when faced with situations that you cannot handle, rather than trying to be a copy-cat.

CHAPTER THREE

THE CALL TO MINISTRY

*"**Known** unto **God** are all **His** works from the beginning of the world."*

Acts 15:18

Whilst in Lagos, I was a member of the Surulere Baptist Church which was under Mr. E. K Jones. When the pastor saw my enthusiasm for the work of God, he asked me to assist him and I began to preach frequently and, soon, I grew to become the Sunday school superintendent.

The church was a stone throw from where I lived in Surulere, so I did not need to go to First Baptist Church, Broad Street, which was the other option. Apart from that, the Surulere Baptist Church needed somebody who had experience in church administration since the pastor was there in an acting capacity and was not trained. The pastor and members wanted me to do what I could, to assist the church to grow better. I did not know the zeal I showed then would become a blessing in disguise for me. The time for Sunday services in those days were advertised in Saturday newspapers, so also was the name of the preacher for that day, which was either E.K. Jones or W.R.O. Ojo. Even before I became a pastor, many people in the church had started calling me a pastor already because I was spiritually blessed and I had a good knowledge of the Bible. As time went by, I began getting more and more involved in the administration of the church and the call to become a pastor remained pervasive. While I was rendering my services to the church I also continued with my work at the Nigerian Railways but I became fed up with my job because of the way superiors treated their subordinates.

The way junior workers were treated left much to be desired and in my heart. I saw that the younger staffs did not like being referred to as messengers. While others were comfortable tossing them around like slaves and calling them demeaning names, I called them by their real names and I discovered that it was helpful because they were ever ready to help me anytime that I needed any form of assistance. As though some members of the church knew that I was getting fed up with my job, they began to tell me that they loved my sermons and suggested that I go for theological training. I got drawn more and more to the work of God and when I could not stand the inadequacies of the environment at work, I heeded the call to become a pastor and resigned from the Nigerian Railway Corporation in January, 1952. I prayed to God about it. I knew I was ready and prepared to serve Him but what I was not prepared for was the reaction of my girlfriend to what I felt would be an innocuous decision.

Baptist Theological Seminary, Ogbomoso: 1952-1955

> "Seest thou a man diligent in his business? He shall stand before kings; he shall not stand before mean men."
>
> — *Proverbs 22:29 KJV*

After working for three years in Lagos, first at the Electricity Corporation of Nigeria (ECN), and later at the Nigerian Railway Corporation, I was still unfulfilled and I had a longing for God's work. I resigned my job and decided to head for the Baptist Theological Seminary[2] to be trained as a pastor. I was already the Sunday School Superintendent and a frequent preacher at the Surulere Baptist Church where I was worshiping when I got to Lagos. It was to fill the urge of serving God whole-heartedly that I decided in January 1952 to quit my job and head for the seminary.

Journey to Priesthood

The educational qualification for gaining entry into the Seminary for the Bachelor of Theology degree programme was a Grade II Teachers certificate or a London Matriculation Examination Certificate. I chose the 4-year programme since I was qualified. Those with Secondary School Certificates were also admitted but for the diploma programmes. Before the final admission, oral and written interviews were conducted but I took the oral test only, which I passed convincingly. Thereafter, I prepared to resume in the seminary at Ogbomoso by getting all the things I would need at the school. I travelled by lorry to the seminary in January 1952 and it was a long but exciting journey. Fortunately for me, the lorry stopped for me in front of the seminary gate, so that I did not have to drag my things from the lorry into another taxi.

Six of us were admitted; Oteh and Igwe came from Baptist College, Iwo, so they knew themselves. Akande came from Ghana. He is an Ogbomosho man but his parents lived in Ghana and the Baptist mission there was sponsoring him. He would later become the General Secretary of the Baptist Convention. There was also Paul Ebhomielen. Like me, he had

---

2 https://en.wikipedia.org/wiki/Special:WhatLinksHere/The_Nigerian_Baptist_Theological_Seminary

a London Matriculation Certificate plus Teachers Certificate and was a headmaster in a school in the old Mid-Western State. There was also Osadolor Imasogie who would later be the best man at my wedding.

Of the six of us, I was the only one who had financial constraint. Surulere Baptist Church where I had served prior to my coming to the seminary could not assist me. Unlike the Ghana Baptist Mission, it did not have the financial and leadership capacity to do so. Imasogie, Igwe, Oteh and Ebhomielen were sponsored by the Baptist missions in their home states. I could not get any sponsors from my own home state because there was no Baptist work yet in Igbara-Oke, nevertheless, I was determined to forge ahead. Initially, I did not have problems because I was able to make use of the money I had saved while I was working in Lagos. The school fees was moderate and the seminary provided most of the textbooks we needed. More importantly, the library was adequately equipped and I did not need much money at the start. As God would have it, a fellow student, S.A. Lawanson from Ilesa who heard that I had worked in the civil service referred me to the Baptist Mission Builder, Rev. B.E. Cockrum, to work with him. I got the job as his typist and later worked on his accounts. After working with him for few weeks, he recommended me to Dr. J.C. Pool, the Seminary Principal who needed more help in the Seminary office.

Many people believed that I was an indigene of Lagos because of my outlook. Those at the seminary called me 'Lagos man' because of the way I dressed which was quite different from how others did. I also had my Rudge bicycle that had speed control and light, which was a big possession in those days. Apart from the bicycle, I also brought with me to the seminary, an iron bed, a mattress and two pillows.

The seminary was no place to have fun: you could tell this from the environment and the lecturers. The evidence that we were in for serious work was demonstrated to us on the day we resumed because we began studies immediately. All the classrooms in the seminary were labelled and different categories of courses were taught in the seminary. The degree programme was taught by white missionaries like Dr J.C. Pool, Dr. P.H. Hill, Dr. J.E. Humphries, Dr. W.L. Jester, Dr. R.L. West and Rev. W. Gilliland, because there were no qualified African Theology graduates who could teach at that level at that time. Africans were only allowed to handle programmes in the vernacular and certificate classes.

Since we were just six in class, I had a very cordial relationship with my colleagues throughout my stay in the seminary. Two of us were married already and the seminary provided accommodation for them in the Married apartments, to accommodate their wives and children. Of the remaining four of us who were single, I would, eventually, be the first to get married after graduation.

I enjoyed my stay in the Seminary particularly because of my closeness to the principal, Dr. J.C. Pool. I was placed on an appreciable allowance which was helpful to me for as long as I worked in his office. Apart from that, I had the privilege to work at my own convenience so it did not affect my studies. A log-book was provided for me to record the hours I worked and what time I came in and left. When Dr. Pool later got to know that I had worked at the Electricity Corporation of Nigeria, he made sure that it was my duty, whenever we were going to pay electricity and water bills, to get the task done.

There were about 50 churches in and around Ogbomoso at that time and most of them were assigned student-pastors. I was assigned to Baaki

Baptist Church for a year and it was there that I met Mr. J.B. Ojo (who would later become a chief), the church secretary, who welcomed me warmly. The seminary provided each student-pastor outside Ogbomoso town with a bicycle but I offered to use mine. We were expected to conduct two services in the church on Sunday mornings and Sunday evenings. The morning service was for the students and staffs of the school in Baaki and the evening service was for those who missed the morning service, either because they had to be on the farm or they had other engagements. One Sunday, after the morning service, Mr. Ojo called me and said he did not like how I was shuttling in the morning and in the evening, between the seminary and Baaki. He suggested that I should be resting at his place at the end of the morning service.

I accepted his offer and from that time on, not only did he offer his house as a place of rest, he provided food for me to eat also. We went together on visitations to some members of the church and because of this, the church kept growing and that made the entire church to like us. Our friendship grew stronger also and at the end of that year, we managed to put up a Baptist Day School. At that time, it was the churches that paid the teachers because government was having lots of difficulties getting money to pay them. With the grace of God, we were able to rebuild the school and pay the teachers' salaries.

After one year, I observed that the Baptist Training Union needed attention because it had been in neglect for a long time. I felt it could be resuscitated and I asked for the permission of the seminary faculty to do so for my remaining years in the seminary. I was given the go-ahead to do all I could and to the glory of God, I was able to do quite a lot by organizing courses for fellow students in the seminary. One of the advantages of the Baptist Training Union was that it gave students the opportunity to stand and speak before a large audience. Many students had their first experience in public speaking at the Training Union. During training, students were expected to develop points for discussion and were taken through drilling exercises in all manner of speeches. The Training Union helped many students to overcome their shyness and whatever incapacity they had.

When I was winding up my programme at the seminary, I encouraged my friend, J.B. Ojo, to go to the College of Education to obtain a Grade II Teacher Training Certificate because I saw that he wanted to be well-educated. He was a pupil teacher already but I wanted him to study more. He entered for a two-year course at the Elementary Training Centre (ETC) in Ede. At the same time, he sought admission to the Baptist College, Iwo, for a four-year course. As fate would have it, the result of Ede came out first but all the money he had was not enough for him to go off to Ede for the two-year course. He was downbeat but I told him to go ahead and that we would look for a way to solve the problem. While we were still thinking of a way round that, the result from the entrance exam he wrote to be admitted to Iwo arrived. He was now torn between going for a two-year and a four-year course. He became so confused because there was no money to pursue any of the two admissions. When he sought my advice, I told him to go for the four-year course and insisted that he start with the little money he had. I was sure that God would bail us out. With faith, he opted for the four-year course. There were difficulties initially but by the time he got to the third year, I was already doing well and was able to give some help. J.B. Ojo had been a succour to me in time past and if the Lord would grant me grace to be of assistance to him in my little way, I counted it a privilege to be of help also, and I did with all joy! That was how he was able to get his Grade II Teachers Certificate from the Baptist College. He remained a true friend to me. The same scenario played itself out once more when he had to go to the University of Ibadan. Things were a little better by then but he could not pay the fee. Again I encouraged him to go ahead and start the programme. By God's grace, he finished the programme and became a graduate teacher. He went on to become a principal and when he retired, he was made a chief in Ogbomoso, his hometown.

I learnt a lot from the Baptist ministers in Ogbomoso. They had one striking attribute and that is the love they had for the work of God. Their dedicated service to God is one attribute that, today, is lacking in many pastors and men of God. The Ogbomoso ministers never craved their own comfort but that of other people. For example, Rev. S.A. Ige was in one pastorate throughout his service life. He served in the same church – Ijero Baptist Church for 69 years! His sermons were always short but had far-reaching meanings. Until he died, he was an upright man and he fought against every evil. There was one deity called *Atinga* in Ogbomoso and it came out only at certain periods of the year. Indigenes, particularly women, were not allowed to go out during its celebration but in one year when the idol was going to be celebrated, Rev. Ige defied all the odds. He said he could no longer stay at home and urged people to go about their businesses without fear. People did as he directed and pandemonium broke out between the idol worshippers and Christians. During the chaos, one of the worshippers was injured and it became big trouble. Revd. Ige stood by his action when the matter was taken before the ruling council, insisting that Ogbomoso must accept Christ and be rid of all idols. Surprisingly, he won the case and nothing was done to him. In the history of *Atinga* idol, Rev. Ige's name will continue to be remembered because of his boldness. We all had so much respect for him because of his simplicity. He had just one house and that was where he stayed until he died. In the history of the Baptist Convention, he was the longest serving pastor in a pastorate.

Another minister I admired very much was Rev. Adediran. He was from Ogbomoso too. He was one of the founders of First Baptist Church, Oke Elerin, and the oldest church in Ogbomoso. Papa Adediran was also dedicated to the course of Christ. His daughter was returning home from Ibadan one day and just before Ogbomoso, she had an accident and died instantly. The whole of Ogbomoso received the news with shock and how to break the news to Papa Adediran, who was away in Saki, became a debate. It was later agreed that he should be tricked home from Saki. When he got home, he observed that things were very unusual and he asked those around why there was a bizarre calmness around his home. Nobody could brave it to tell him what had just happened until one of the elderly Reverends summoned the courage to tell him the terrible news of his daughter's death. After he was told, what came out of his mouth threw many of us off balance. All he said was, *"It is the Lord who giveth and it is Him who taketh."* His daughter was a very young and bright woman but the man never betrayed any emotions. He was a strong man that I came to admire and I learnt so much from him, and, from that incident.

There was Baba Odebunmi also, who made a good impression on me when his faith was tested. He handled the matter calmly and maturely. I left the Seminary in 1955 to continue my journey in life, this time, my first pastorate work in First Baptist Church, Igede, Ekiti.

Baptist Theological Seminary, Ogbomosho

CHAPTER FOUR

TWO BODIES, ONE SOUL

"Whoso findeth a wife findeth a good thing, and obtaineth favour of the LORD."

— *Proverbs 18:22 KJV*

My First Shot

Although Igbara-Oke was a village, it was not short of many beautiful women. To have a girlfriend then did not require material wealth, all you needed was to identify a particular girl you liked and make your intentions known to her. Though there were so many young and beautiful girls in the town to pick from, I lived all my teenage years without a girlfriend because I did not consider it very important at that point in time. Showing commitment was one of the attributes of keeping a relationship but I made up my mind that my commitment would be to my education and how I would become successful in life, first. I had many family friends, male and female who were engaged to one another but I was not moved by that. Nonetheless, my desire to remain single did not change until I got admission into the B.B.H.S. Abeokuta where I met the girl who would be my first girlfriend. Mobola was a niece of a Baptist Pastor's wife but she was treated like a daughter. She was in Girls' Mission School, Idi Aba, while I was at B.B.H.S. The trend then was that boys from B.B.H.S chose their girlfriends from the girls' school in Idi-Aba since it was like a sister-school. It also had some of the most beautiful girls in town which made just a few of us to never think of having our girlfriends in other girls' schools. Since missionaries were in charge of both schools, we shared a lot of things in common. For example, our open days fell on the same day and this always created a very good opportunity for the boys from B.B.H.S. to visit the girls in Idi-Aba.

Our visit to Idi-Aba was always a big issue amongst ourselves and we always planned ahead in case we needed to buy anything for our girlfriends. The visit to Idi-Aba was one of the privileges senior students had because they were allowed a level of freedom and accorded a degree of respect beyond what other classes enjoyed. On the part of the girls, they too were always expectant of our visit because that was their only chance of getting to see us as they were not allowed to leave their school premises except they had academic engagements. On the day of our visits, we were usually hosted in the common room where we would all sit and send one of the girls to call whom we had come to see. Once they appeared in the common room, the ambience of the whole place would change and smiles would immediately take over the faces of everyone, and in no time, the room would be a flurry of activities till it was time to take our exit.

We did not go beyond talking during any of our visits because moral values were high, which made it almost impossible for male and female students to mess up with each other since the girls had been taught to act safe and to avoid being tricked into having premarital sex. For this reason, it became almost impracticable for them to be lured or cajoled into something destructive. Missionary schools, particularly, were very strict concerning moral vices but some grammar schools and government-run schools were relaxed in their rules as they placed less emphasis on how male and female students related with one another.

I dated Mobola for four years and during those years, we were the envy of my classmates and all others who knew us to be friends. We went out during the holidays and most especially, Mobola's aunt always made sure that I took my girlfriend to the cinema hall whenever she was in Lagos to visit them. In spite of this, her aunt always admonished us to be careful and not be tempted into doing what we would regret in life. Indeed, we remained faithful to each other and it made our relationship to grow stronger. As my desire to serve God grew, so did my fondness for Mobola. Serving God meant a lot to me and she knew of the role I was playing in the Surulere Baptist Church, but she never set her sight or mind on the likelihood that I would one day become a full time pastor.

As time went on, it became apparent that all I wanted to become was an ordained pastor and that could mean me going to the Baptist Seminary for training. As the vision became clearer, I stepped up my prayers to God to fulfil His purpose for my life. Then sometime in 1951, I called Mobola and told her that I wanted to leave my job at the Nigerian Railways and go to the seminary to train as a priest. Immediately I dropped the news, silence enveloped the air and shock was written all over her face. When she opened her mouth to say something, minutes after the quiet had drowned all the noise around us, Mobola told me in very simple language that she was not ready to be a pastor's wife. I was shocked by her response but I tried all I could to convince her that there was nothing wrong in being a pastor's wife. All entreaties to her after then was like a man trying to build a wall with tennis balls.

It was as if something hit me that day and very quickly, sadness and despair took over me, such that for a long time to come I could not bring myself to terms with the fact that Mobola had actually left me. On their own, her guardians, the Pastor and his wife – her aunt – tried all they could to make sure we reconciled our differences but Mobola was insistent and she was not ready to compromise. I kept on wondering why someone who had lived with, and was brought up by a pastor, would feel so uncomfortable with her boyfriend wanting to become a pastor. I kept on thinking for days why she would detest the fact that I wanted to serve God even with the fact that her father, Pa. Laosebikan was an educationist and a very religious man.

When I tried all I could to win her back and all my efforts proved unproductive, I decided to carry my cross and bear the burden alone because my mind was irreversibly made up and there was no turning back on my decision to go to the seminary to train to become a pastor. That dream was already signed and sealed, not only on earth, but in heaven, and I decided from that moment on, that not even Mobola, as much as I loved her and did not want to lose her, or even my father whose influence on me was great, could prevent me from becoming a priest. I found it hard to move on because I did not want to believe that the relationship that was built in four years had come to an abrupt end because of an innocuous decision I took. Although my heart was broken, my dream of going to the seminary was still alive.

To the Seminary I Went
I entered the seminary in 1952 still feeling sad and blue because it was not easy erasing Mobola's memory from my heart. Once I had settled in at the seminary, I met Rev. Gollilard who became a good friend and a mentor to me. He assisted me a great deal in trying to move on with my life after I told him how my heart was broken. Despite his comforting

words, I still nursed a fondness for Mobola. I kept a tab on her to know how and what she was doing, but that would not be for long because she left Lagos to become a teacher in a town in Oyo State and I received the shocking news that she had gone into another relationship. When we met years later, she apologized for everything and asked me to be the officiating minister at her daughter's wedding; a request I granted, to her admiration.

The Bone of My Bones

> *"This is now bone of my bones, and flesh of my flesh: she shall be called Woman, because she was taken out of Man. Therefore shall a man leave his father and his mother, and shall cleave unto his wife: and they shall be one flesh."*
>
> *- Genesis 2:23B-24 KJV*

After Rev. Gollilard counselled me on why I needed to forget about Mobola, he prayed with me and told me to believe that God will certainly give me the bone of my bones. That bone of my bones turned out to be somebody I had known for many years. As a matter of fact, it was somebody I grew up with in Igbara-Oke. Biodun Aloba and I had been very good friends in Igbara-Oke and he accommodated me when I first visited Lagos. He was the only son of the Aloba family and had many younger sisters. One of them was Grace and she was my very good friend, though I was a little older than her. Their parents and mine were very good friends because we all went to the same church and our houses were two houses from each other on the same side of the same street. For this reason, we had the freedom to visit each other but it never crossed my mind then that

I would get married to somebody I knew so well, and whose family was very close to mine.

Grace had an older sister, Tinuola (who became Mrs. Ehigie) and a younger sister Bosede (Professor (Mrs.) Sophie Oluwole) from their mother. Their father was a polygamist and he had children from his other wives. At a time, Grace left Igbara-Oke to stay with some of their relatives in Benin but providentially, after two years she returned, but her education had been badly affected. She insisted that she was not going to go to school anymore because her younger sister, Bosede was now ahead of her and some of her classmates were now teachers. No one could convince her to return to school. During one of my visits to their home, I asked what she would like to do in life. She said she wanted to sew dresses, among other things. I asked her if the education she had was enough for her to take clients' measurements accurately, cut the fabrics and sew properly. She said 'no'. I said to her, "Don't you think it will be wise to get more education to be able to measure, cut and sew properly in order to avoid getting your sewing wrong and getting into customer's troubles?" She said 'yes' and with that she was convinced and went back to the primary school and anytime she needed help, I made sure that I was always around to help her without any ulterior motive. It did not cross my mind at that time, however, that I would later get married to Grace. Fortunately for Grace, some years later, she passed the Standard Six examinations and was admitted into the Teacher Training College, Ilesa, the same year with Bosede. While Bosede chose to study elementary education, Grace opted for domestic science. We kept communicating while she was away and immediately she graduated, she was posted to Ondo Girl's School where she taught for a couple of years. At this time I had gone off to the seminary and after a year or two, she was transferred to Ikare.

My Rising Affection

My affection for Grace began to grow later, in the seminary, and I remember visiting her once in Ondo. Anytime I was in Igbara-Oke, Grace always came with me wherever I went and it did not take long for the love to develop. I was home on holidays one time and I told her point blank that I was interested in her. It was very easy to tell her because I saw that she was very supportive of my becoming a pastor. When I proposed to her, she was not shocked. She liked the idea of both of us starting a relationship but she asked that I gave her time to pray about it. After a while, we made up our minds and agreed that we were truly meant for each other. We were engaged for about three years and during those years, I was at peace with myself. I had long told her about Mobola and what I went through when she decided to leave me. Grace became the panacea that I needed to cure the painful effect of Mobola leaving me.

Gaining acceptance from Grace's family was not a problem. Her parents, Chief Timothy and Mama Comfort Aloba (nee Oni) had been good friends of my family in Igbara-Oke. I had their support and friendship all the way. They were so happy with the fact that it was not a 'stranger' their daughter wanted to marry. When I told my father that I was interested in marrying Grace, he too was very happy. I remember him saying it had been his prayer that I married somebody he knew very well. There was not so much fanfare about relationships at that time. It was only the few times I had the opportunity of seeing her that we talked. I usually did most of the visiting since I was well known by her family. We loved exchanging gifts especially at anniversaries or during church calendar activities.

Eternal Union

Grace Modupe Aloba and I got engaged in 1954. It was a very quiet

Chief Timothy Aloba – my father in law. *Chief Mrs Comfort Aloba – my mother in law*

occasion. Our marriage was planned for the following year when I would have rounded off my study at the seminary. I purposely did not want to get married while I was still in the seminary because it would disturb my studies. Coupled with that, I did not have enough money to spend for the wedding ceremonies. Things were tight at the seminary but because of the little money I was being paid while working in the principal's office, I was able to take care of some things on my own. Since I did not want to finish at the seminary and go to the church without a wife, we planned that we would get married following my graduation, in December of 1955.

My desire had been to get married before I became an ordained pastor because the work is not a one-man job. Being single and doing pastoral work has many challenges. For example, some female members may come to you for counselling about an issue that a woman would handle better. Having a wife makes it easier. Also a male pastor who is single risks being suspected of amorous affairs if he is found in the company of women too often. I concluded that if I had my own wife, the suspicion of anything untoward would be automatically checked. The Bible also establishes that it is not good for a man to be alone and there is a whole lot of truth in that statement. Though there are single men who are pastors and are doing well, I believe that being married enables you to do more work, especially if you have a good wife who lifts you up in prayers, gives you good support and wise counsel in all your endeavours. I was prepared physically for marriage but not financially. All I had was the bicycle I had ridden in Lagos before coming to the seminary, so I took a loan from the seminary for my wedding which I later paid back in 1956, after I had worked and saved some money.

Our Walk down the Isle

Our wedding took place at St. Paul's Anglican Church, Igbara-Oke on December 22, 1955. There were so many priests at the wedding. Anglican and Baptist ministers including Rev. J.C. Poll and Rev. S.O. Makanjuola were in charge of proceedings on that day. Many family members and friends came from far and wide to Igbara-Oke. It was one sweet day for us. My sister, Sarah, played a very prominent part in making sure that everything went well. Grace was very happy on that day: the look on her face said it all. Both of us did not need anybody to tell us that we were made for each other. She looked so resplendent in her wedding gown that my heart kept on saying to me; "you have made the right choice."

My Best Man was Osadolor Imasogie, my classmate at the seminary. He was from Benin and because of our closeness and the fact that he came from my wife's place, I did not think twice before I asked him to be my Best Man. He knew my wife's family had ties with Benin and he showed more interest especially because of that. A tailor in Ibadan called Fisher, made our suits. Fisher was a very competent tailor and he sewed in such a way that you could boast that any clothes he made for you were made in England. Osadolor was single and my in-laws took to him immediately they got to know he was from Benin. Grace on her own part chose one of her good friends, Shade Fajemisin as her Chief Bridesmaid.

That day will forever be memorable. My father, a natural crowd-puller made sure our people came from Ere and Ijebu-Ijesa, where my grandmother hails from. My wife's relatives also came from Benin to Igbara-Oke in large numbers. A few of my friends from Lagos and the seminary also turned up. Peter Obe of *Daily Times* was the official photographer and it was through him that the wedding pictures were featured later in the *Daily Times*. We did not have a huge party after the

Climbing the steps to the Church are L-R Osadolor Imasogie, Abiodun Aloba, Grace and Shade Fajemisin

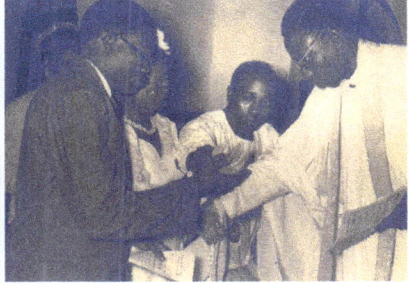

Some family and friends

Page boys – Dipo & Akin Aloba, Fehinti Ehigie

Bridal train, family and friends

L-R – Sister Sarah, Mama Comfort Aloba and bridal train

At the wedding reception

church service because we were leaving for Igede that same day. Our wedding cake was made in Lagos. My friend and wife's brother, Abiodun Aloba was wonderful throughout the ceremony. After the ceremonies, my wife and I headed to Igede to begin our first assignment. I had looked forward to getting married and through God's grace, I knew I would enjoy it.

A Marriage of Roses
My first months of marriage were quite interesting. You woke up at night to find a woman by your side. It was quite interesting. We shared so many things in common. There wasn't so much to do when we first got to Igede. My wife was always away at school while I was either at home or in the office doing something for the Ondo Baptist Association, the church, or the high school. My wife has been supportive ever since we got married. At times when things were difficult, she always understood and gave a helping hand.

We were both virgins when we got married. Our first challenge was that of conception. It took us some years before we achieved our first pregnancy. All went well until the time of delivery. My wife laboured for five days and I became afraid because she was in so much pain. By the time the baby eventually came, he just took a short breath and gave up. Our very first child did not live long. Looking back now I realise that we lost him due to the negligence of the medical personnel who handled the delivery. It was a painful and sad loss to us and our families, nevertheless, we did not allow the incident to distract us. Instead, we continued hoping in God for better days ahead. Not long after, my wife got pregnant again and we were totally overjoyed. This time, we took all the necessary precautions and made sure that we did not take any chances. We called on God day and night to take control of everything during the pregnancy and the delivery. This time around just as my wife was being wheeled on a stretcher to the theatre, our son came out! It was so emotional for all that the Doctor used the prepared theatre drape to wrap him up first. By God's grace, she had a safe and sound delivery. When we began having our children, we decided to give them names that had meanings that would resonate with the family, particularly to my wife and I. In those days however, it was the responsibility of the grandparents, if they were still around, to name the first child of their children, therefore our first son was named Durojaiye in agreement with our desire to give him a native name. Nevertheless, he had other names that were given to him from his maternal family.

Our joy knew no bounds when Durojaiye was born. The news of my wife's safe delivery was that of joy to the whole town. With the blessings of God, we did all we could to make sure our son enjoyed the best of care and attention. My wife was a Domestic Science teacher at the Baptist Modern School, Igede-Ekiti and anytime she was going to school, she always wheeled 'Jaiye with her in a mobile cot. The students were always happy. They always wanted to touch and carry him. They loved him so much. Fifteen months later, when 'Kemi too was born, the whole town was thrown into a joyous mood again. They loved our two children very much and till today, they still refer to them as indigenes of Igede-Ekiti. We had another daughter named Bunmi but she died in Jos, when she contacted measles. Again, she died due to medical negligence. We had another son named Deji and he too died in Abeokuta, again, due to medical negligence. Then came another daughter, Oluremilekun, born in Abeokuta, and two other sons, Dapo and Supo were born in Ibadan some years later. We prayed to God for children, we expected, and the Lord gave them to us. We always see them as God's doing. We lost three but today to the Glory of God alone, we have five children. We thank God because they are all doing well in their chosen fields. The fact that their mother was a school teacher and I an un-certificated teacher, helped in bringing up the children. They fitted easily into everything. We taught them far more than what any ordinary child would ever learn. Our children had the best of spiritual and academic education.

CHAPTER FIVE

TRIALS AND TRIUMPHS

"These things I have spoken unto you, that in me ye might have peace. In the world ye shall have tribulation: but be of good cheer; I have overcome the world."

John 16:33 KJV

"In righteousness shalt thou be established: thou shalt be far from oppression; for thou shalt not fear: and from terror; for it shall not come near thee. Behold, they shall surely gather together, but not by me: whosoever shall gather together against thee shall fall for thy sake. Behold, I have created the smith that bloweth the coals in the fire, and that bringeth forth an instrument for his work; and I have created the waster to destroy. No weapon that is formed against thee shall prosper; and every tongue that shall rise against thee in judgment thou

> *shalt condemn. This is the heritage of the servants of the Lord, and their righteousness is of me, saith the Lord."*
>
> *Isaiah 54:14-17 KJV*

Right from my childhood, I had always enjoyed good health. There was never a time I fell so ill that it became impossible for me to go out until sometime in 1982. It all started with a simple headache that would not go away. I saw the family doctor who gave me some medications, asked me to take some time off work and suggested that I should stop drinking coffee. These were all done to no avail. Later in that period, I did not know anything. My head was blank. I had no strength. It became very difficult for me, even to move. It got to a point that I did not know where I was and for how long, and could only barely recognise Sister Sarah, my wife and children.

My family and all the people who heard that I was ill began praying for my quick recovery. At a point, my family approached some of the top officials of the Convention on my behalf. They wanted the Convention to do something as quickly as possible regarding getting me abroad for treatment. My family and friends were praying as well as the missionaries in Ogbomoso, who formed a prayer chain to pray for me every hour of the day and night. I got to know all these after I got better.

One of my friends, Professor Okedara, came to visit me at the hospital once, and when he was leaving he told my wife that he would never set foot in the hospital again. He said he would rather be praying for me to get out of the sickness. According to him, he could neither stand the sight nor bear the condition he saw me in, when he came visiting. Another of my friends also told me after I got better, that he had to send someone ahead always, to check if I was still in the bed before he could come and see me in the private ward where I was later put.

When my condition was not improving, my family, in particular Sister Sarah, approached the general secretary of the Convention and the other officials of the Convention were contacted and it was agreed that I should be flown abroad for better medical services. The Convention was ready to bear all the expenses as long as it would restore my health. My family was contacted and advised to discuss with my consultant so that he could make all the necessary arrangements for me to be flown out of the country. My doctor did not object but only asked that they give him a little time to conclude some arrangements and he promised to get back to my family. I learnt later that the headaches were so severe that once it came, the whole bed will be shaking and as I had a few falls because of this, they had to put cot sides on my bed. I learnt I had tubes everywhere in and around me. I learnt that I was moved from the main ward to a private side room. At that time in the University College Hospital (UCH), Ibadan, relatives were not allowed to stay with ward patients outside the visiting times and certainly not at night.

On a particular night, after over six weeks that I had been more or less in a coma, and unaware of where I was and for how long, as I would learn later, something strange and miraculous happened. I experienced an unusual warmth from my toes, working its way up to my head, though I was in coma. Although I was fast asleep, a voice kept urging me to get up from the bed and I kept wondering where the voice was coming from. I remained rooted to the same spot. Moreover I had all kinds of medical tubes fixed to my body and I could not move. The second time, the same voice called out that I should get up but I still lay on the bed, baffled, because I could not get up. The order came mildly again and this time, the voice gave me some instructions to open my eyes first. I did and when I looked around me, it did not look like my home or a guest house, assuming that I had travelled. Immediately I had to figure out where this could be and realised that it must be a hospital. The next question was, "Which hospital?" My family would probably only bring me to UCH, Ibadan. What is wrong with me and for how long have I been here? I had no idea. Then the voice instructed me to raise each leg up one by one and put them down, raise each arm up one by one and put them down, lift up my head from the pillow and put it down, sit up in the bed and come down from the bed and walk. I felt something like a power surge inside me. I obeyed and managed to move from my bed towards the wall but I could not get to it because of the tubes. At that point, the burst of energy inside me had increased but I could not move farther than where I was. For the first time in a long while, I stood up unaided. I kept wondering what was happening. The voice said I could lay down on my bed again. I laid back slowly on the bed with some form of glee in my heart. Something great had happened to me. That much I knew!

Early the next morning as the nurse came in to do the routine blood pressure and ward round, I greeted her but she ran out of my room in a frenzy! The duty matron was called in and I greeted her too. The Consultant, Dr. Adeuja was informed. He came many times that day and asked what had happened, what my family had done and so on. All I could say for the next 24 hours was 'I thank God I am now back.' I told him, "Doctor, would you believe it if I told you that I got up from my bed last night? But for the tubes, I would have moved farther" He was stunned. He did not believe me so I asked him to remove the tubes so that I could demonstrate in his presence, what happened in the night. Reluctantly, he obliged. I managed to get up, took a few steps to the window and walked back again to my bed unaided. The doctor was surprised. It was a moment of respite for him. That much I could tell from the looks on his face. A few days after that glorious incident, my recovery rate became faster than ever before. My wife and children were very happy when they heard the good news. The news spread to the whole Baptist Convention that I was now recuperating. All the plans that were being made by my family and the Convention to fly me abroad became unnecessary. Until now, I am unable to explain where the voice came from. I know that it could only have been the Voice of God or that of an angel of God. I remember that I heard a strange voice instructing me to rise from the bed and walk. Everybody who heard the news of my glorious healing became elated at what the Lord did for me. My family and I held a thanksgiving service sometime later for the miraculous healing. However, it was not yet time to retire, at least from serving God. 'For this God is our God for ever and ever; he will be our guide even to the end **(Psalms 48:14 NIV)**."

Some years later, out of nowhere, I experienced a surgical problem and needed to undergo surgery at the University College Hospital (UCH), Ibadan. UCH at that time was not technologically advanced as it would later be, but the professionalism of doctors, nurses, radiographers, laboratory technologists etc. at the hospital was unparalleled. My wife and children agreed with the doctors that surgery was the best thing to do if I was to continue enjoying a good health. A few months after I was diagnosed of the ailment and admitted to the hospital, the surgery took place. For the surgery to take place however, the hospital required that several pints of blood be donated and available in the hospital's blood bank in case there was need for blood transfusion during or after the surgery. The Baptist Convention was immediately notified and without delay, they swung into action. Surprisingly a missionary from America, Miss Betty McQueen, was the first to volunteer to donate some blood. She told me later, that her decision to donate her blood was because the Bible established firmly that the Lord created everybody with the same blood and she did not see any reason why she could not donate her blood to a fellow human being. After she donated, other people volunteered too. I had the goodwill and the support of many people. My belly was slit open for the surgery. I don't know what went on during the operation but with God's help, I came out of it alive. Though the operation was efficiently carried out by Professor E.O. Nkposong and his team of surgeons to the best of their abilities, the painful experience I had after the operation is beyond description. When I was fully fit to go home, I was discharged but was asked to come for medical check-ups and dressing. God healed me totally and rapidly too. At this juncture, I will like to appreciate all mothers, especially those who give birth to their children through surgery.

CHAPTER SIX

FROM STATION TO STATION

"Also I heard the voice of the Lord, saying, whom shall I send, and who will go for us? Then said I, Here am I; send me."

- Isaiah 6:8

When I decided to become a priest, I sought and got the full support and total backing of my father. He never doubted my ability to go all the way in whatever I chose to do, neither did he question my decision; all he told me was that I should remain steadfast and upright. He only wished that I became an Anglican priest instead of a Baptist one. Like him, one of my aunts would also have preferred me to join the Anglican clergy. She hinged her own reason on the fact that Baptist pastors did not wear collars and robes like their Anglican counterparts. Nevertheless, when they saw that I was very keen on becoming a Baptist and not an Anglican priest as they wished, they relented and gave me the support that I needed. My father loved people serving God and he used to say, "Being a pastor gives one peace of mind."

Not surprisingly, when Baptist missionary work was going to take off in

Igbara-Oke and I asked that he allow us to start it in his living room, he did not object. He only stressed that, though he did not mind me doing Baptist work in his house, he was not ready to become a Baptist because he was an elder in the Anglican Church. I assured him that, that would not be a problem and he gave his support to Baptist work until he died in 1982.

Baptist Work in Igbara-Oke

I had my infant baptism in the Anglican Church in Igbara-Oke, had my primary school education and taught in the Anglican community. The first Baptist town I knew was Abeokuta when I was admitted to BBHS as a student in 1944. There was a lot of Baptist work being done in the town and students from Iwo, Ogbomosho, Lagos, Igede and other towns came to the Seminary on sponsorship by their parents, churches or missionaries. I had no such sponsorship, as Igbara-Oke was an Anglican dominated town. Fortunately I met Sam Makanjuola– a final year student from Igede and we became friends. He graduated in 1952 and in 1953 he was posted to serve in Igede. God led him to choose Igbara-Oke as his first preaching station. He started with a few people in my father's house and as the number increased, the group moved to larger accommodation and later to a Church building and they had a Pastor. Other Baptist Pastors who served earlier in Igbara-Oke were F.O. Jemiriye, M.A. Ajakaiye and M.G. Olanrewaju.

Two missionary couples, the J.S. McGees and J.B Hills helped morally and financially, in building a befitting Church. The then Oba, His Royal Highness, Oba Adetiloye and his chiefs as well as His Royal Highness, Oba Asarun were cooperative and generous in providing the land for the Baptist work in Igbara-Oke. J.B. Ojo (Ojo Alawo) and G.E. Makinde, both indigenes of Igbara-Oke were equally financially generous to the Church projects. Deacons Ajewole, Kuye, Makinde, Olaoluwa and Deaconesses Victoria Ayeni and Margret Olofin were ordained on July 20, 1991. My wife and I also gave every possible assistance to the growth of the work and today there are two Baptist Churches and two Baptist schools (one good primary and one secondary) in the town.

My journey from station to station as a pastor, began exactly, on my wedding day on December 22, 1955.

Pastor, First Baptist Church, Igede-Ekiti: 1955-1960

The First Baptist Church, Igede was our (my wife and I) first official place of assignment after leaving the Seminary, though I was yet to be ordained. My wife and I were well received by the people of the town and especially the members of the congregation who accorded us an unforgettable reception. My first pastoral assignment was challenging because I took over from an old pastor who was retiring after doing quite well for the church but with God's wisdom and knowledge, we were able to settle down to face the task ahead of us.

Initially, things were a little rough for Grace and I because we had no place to stay. The old pastoral house was in an uninhabitable state of disrepair and it had no ventilation. In addition, the interior was so dimly lit that even in the afternoon one needed a lamp to see properly. We moved into a rented apartment pending when the repairs of the pastoral house would be completed but we learnt that the landlord had mismanaged government money and was going to be probed. He was found guilty and the government decided they were going to Fi-Fa[38] (pronounced *fai-fe*)

---

38   *Fieri Facias (usually abbreviated Fi-Fa) is a writ ordering a levy on the belongings of a debtor to satisfy the debt. In Nigeria, it is a forceful eviction order that is commonly used to gain vacant possession of a property for the landlord where the tenant has defaulted in paying rents. The bailiff armed with an eviction order from the court, removes the property of the tenant so that the landlord can repossess his property.*

his house. It was a one-storey building and we occupied the upper floor. Some members of the church suggested that we should buy the house since the old pastoral house was yet to be repaired but I objected because I did not want us to be part of such an arrangement. To avoid losing any of our property when government officials came to take over the place, we moved our things to the house of a church member adjacent to ours. When the debate on whether to buy the landlord's house or build a new pastoral house occurred again, we opted for the church having its own pastoral house, members rallied round and we embarked on the project. To the glory of God, the new pastoral house was completed in a very short while.

Not long after we settled down in the new building, I was appointed as secretary of the Board of Governors for Ekiti Baptist High School and I also became a teacher in the local Bible School under Rev. McGee and Mr. John B. Hill. I had quite a good time working with these men because of their dedication to the work of God. A few months after that, I was made an official of the Ondo Baptist Association to help the Body in its quest to spread Baptist mission work in Ondo. Later in 1958, I was elected the recording secretary of the Nigerian Baptist Convention; a post I held for six years. Part of my duties as the recording secretary was to write letters and take care of other correspondences for the Convention; good enough, I had a personal typewriter which made my job very easy and helped the Convention to save funds.

At Igede, the day usually began with daily devotion, after which I would have my breakfast and get ready for the day's tasks. As the Pastor of the church, I was expected to be prepared at every point in time because members could call me anytime for one reason or the other. When I saw that things were improving, we introduced adult education in the church to teach grown-up members of the church how to read, particularly the Bible, and to write. When that aspect of the work improved, the church decided to make it a policy to never baptize anyone who could not read the Bible properly. We thank God that by the time we were leaving in 1960, many indigenes of the town could read and write satisfactorily and it gladdened our hearts so much. Whenever we look back, we always thank God for the things we were able to achieve in Igede, despite the fact that I served as a pastor for almost two years without being ordained!

Ordination

When we graduated from the seminary in 1955, some people said we should not be ordained immediately because we had academic experience only, without any field experience. In the past, ordination of new pastors took place immediately or a few months after graduation from the seminary, however, when we graduated in 1955, we were told we were too inexperienced to be ordained. We were asked to proceed to the field, pending when a date would be chosen for our ordination. Since there was little or nothing we could do about it, we left for our different postings with the promise that our ordination would take place in no distant future.

After almost two years of service in Igede, I was ordained as a priest on October 13, 1957. Before ordination in the Baptist Convention, you are required to take both oral and written examinations. Those who had degrees already, sat for the oral examination while those without degrees, but who have had many years of pastoral experience, took the written and oral examinations. In my case and that of five others who graduated with me that year, we took the oral test only, which we all passed. The six of us were ordained in the same year but on different dates because delegates from the Baptist Convention had to be present

Ordination October 13th 1957

at each ceremony. At the convenience of the church in Igede, October 13, 1957 was chosen as my day of ordination.

Prior to the day I was ordained, the Convention sent an ordination committee to Igede to see our level of preparedness and to liaise with the local organizing committee on how to have a hitch-free ordination. When the committee was satisfied with our level of readiness, they gave their nod for the ceremony to go on. In attendance that day were, Dr. I.N. Patterson, Dr. J.T. Ayorinde, Rev. N.F. Fatunla, Dr. E.A. Dahunsi and Rev. S.O. Makanjuola. The atmosphere was so enthralling, as people came from far and wide, especially our families and friends from Igbara-Oke. In the course of the service, somebody stood up to read the recommendation of the ordaining and presiding pastor and thereafter, someone else told the congregation that I had completed my studies at the seminary, gone through oral tests, lived an exemplary life and had passed every test, therefore, I was ready for ordination.

After the recommendation and commendation, someone rose from the congregation to move the motion for my ordination saying, "On behalf of the church, we accept the recommendation of the ordaining council and we want our pastor to be ordained." The motion was then seconded, after which the ordination committee asked the church, "All in favour?" And the whole church chanted in unison, "Yes". The 'yes' I received that day was deafening and glorious. The endorsement brought me glee such that I could not contain my joy and happiness. Subsequent to the endorsement, scriptures were read from the Bible and a special anthem was rendered. After the hymn, one of the ministers admonished the church, my family and I, to make sure we continued to uphold God's ministry. The minister asked the church to give me their support by saying, "You have called him to serve you and you have said you want him to be ordained. You should support him with your prayers, advice, finances and take good care of him. He is a man of God and he must not suffer."

The admonition to my family and I was that, we should not see the church as our personal property. We were told the church was not the building but the people. I was advised on that day to watch out for the three pit falls that could wreck the ministry of a pastor. They were called the 3W's – Wine, Women and Wealth. Wealth, particularly, has destroyed many men of God and so I learnt to never handle church money and to never use dubious ways to get quick money. Many pastors are wont to manipulate church members so that they can get money from them but I never did this. After the ordination, I pronounced the benediction, after which the church presented a Bible to me as a gift, which was signed to signal the day I was ordained.

I preached my first sermon as an ordained pastor the following Sunday, on October 20, 1957 and it centred on obedience to God's words. I shared the message because I wanted the congregation to know that without obeying the word of God, nothing fruitful would come out of life. In every way, my wife and I made sure that we lived an exemplary life so that we would not be misunderstood by the people we were leading.

Onward Christian Soldier
Long after my ordination, I noticed that the church building needed a face-lift, as it was getting old. I informed the church of the need to do something and they gave their approval. However, the church was not financially buoyant enough to execute the project, but I was overwhelmed by the interest and commitment the members showed when they heard of it. They said we could make the plan become a reality through direct

labour, defiantly insisting that the prevailing financial situation must not stop us from putting up a befitting place of worship for the Lord. Immediately I got the nod to go ahead with the work, we went to work and as they promised, the members were always on hand to make cement blocks and do other manual labour. Their efforts helped us in saving cost and we were touched by their resolve to see the project through. Touched because, these were people who did not have money but were willing to give their time. When the building was finally completed, we were all happy to see the labour of our hands standing firm on the ground. Nevertheless, the project did not materialize without hiccups. Some people in Igede became mischievous about what we were doing.

The old church was built in 1901 under the supervision of the Lagos Baptist Convention and this made the building very historic. The first set of pastors to shepherd the church were custodians of history, judging by the way they kept a good account of how and when the church was built, as well as records of attendance at all church services. They also kept a record of the preachers' names, dates of worship, time of service, thanksgiving, birthdays, anniversaries and baptisms, all of which were written for future references. They also had a column in the record book where they wrote their remarks and comments, based on what happened during any of the activities held in the church. It was one of the best churches we served in, where record- keeping was an important aspect of the church and because of that, the people did not joke with the church.

When construction work started, we made sure we used the best building materials, the wood we used would last for as long as 100 years. Although we knew that we did not have much money, we did not want to spare cost, but some people began spreading the rumour that we were using the planks from the old church building to construct the new one. The rumour was so strong that it quickly hit the town that we were short-changing the church by diverting the money meant for the purchase of building materials. The news was greatly disheartening to me and to all those committed to the project but we vowed that we were not going to allow it to disturb us.

Matters got to a head, when one day, I was told that my presence was needed at the Charles Jemiriye Chapel in Igede High School, which incidentally was like the village square. I thought it was a general meeting until I got to the place to find the king of Igede seated already. I was shocked to also find a mammoth crowd at the place and I wondered what was happening. When I looked around, I noticed some faces I recognized, particularly that of one Suberu, who once worked with me. He was a Muslim and he was very popular around Igede. I hid my shock, acknowledged the presence of the king and managed to sit down, still wondering what the huge crowd had come to do. When the conveners of the gathering eventually spoke, they accused me of using old building materials for the new church building that was still under construction. I could not believe my ears, and when I was asked to talk, I stood up, with all eyes transfixed on me. I shook my head, faced the king and told him that I did not know anything about what I was being accused of.

When I managed to look around again, I noticed that many eyes were still piercing at me and the next question I asked those who were accusing me was; "When did Suberu become one of us?" This was somebody I had helped some time ago, who was now taking part with the people who were making unjustifiable allegations against me. Not afraid of what was playing out, I told the king that I had nothing to defend because the entire allegations were untrue. I asked that the king should send people to go and search around the old site, to see if they would not find planks from the old church building neatly placed in one corner of the premises. Convinced in his heart that my accusers had no case against me, the king stood up and strolled away without uttering a word. And one after the other, those who had gathered to see what was going to happen, all left; some, with a look of dejection on their faces. It was a day of victory for me and for the work of God. I became emboldened after that incident and I came to appreciate more, the gracefulness and mercies of God on His children.

My wife and I had quite a good time in Igede even with all the challenges that we faced. Deacons Akande and Oluyeba for instance, were the members of the church who were supportive and stood by me in everything I tried to do. They were deeply religious people and totally committed to the service of God. On another occasion, three other members of the church responded to my call to help rebuild the collapsed bridge between Aramoko and Igede which had been left unrepaired for a long time. The four of us fixed it using our personal finances.

I rode my Rudge bicycle everywhere I went, in my service for God and the people, as a pastor. When it got bad, I requested for a loan to repair it but the church could not come up with the loan. I also used my special typewriter with Yoruba alphabets for the church. I later sold my bicycle and radio, with batteries, to Dare, a member of the church, for 30 pounds. After the church had become firmly rooted and things had taken proper shape, I saw the hand of God and we decided it was time to move on. Because the people had become used to us, they began questioning us on why we wanted to leave, when things were beginning to take shape.

Before we decided it was time to move on, Jos was beckoning that they

IGEDE-EKITI 1955 - 1960

Preparing for service

Water Baptism with Grace ready to give a helping hand

Grace and her Domestic Science Class

Farewell service Igede-Ekiti

wanted me to come and head the First Baptist Church, there. A church member in Jos, Deacon Oyegbile, was sent to woo me and he convinced me about moving to Jos. After I told my wife, she agreed that we could move, though she was also making impact in the town already. She introduced the Domestic Science section in the Baptist Modern School which catered for the home economics needs of the female students. She also led the Women Missionary Union of the church. The church in Igede tried all it could to make us stay but I insisted we had to move on. When we served the church notice that we wanted to leave, they were surprised and we had to keep on telling them that our mission was complete. Moreover, the church could not afford to continue to pay my salary. We moved to Jos in 1961 and continued the work from that point in time.

Pastor, First Baptist Church, Jos: 1961-1963
The three main routes that trains plied in those days were Lagos to Kaduna, Lagos to Port-Harcourt and Lagos to Jos. Trains went from Lagos to Jos twice in a week and the nearest connection point for us was in Osogbo. My wife, Jaiye, Kemi and I, could not leave for Jos on the designated day because of a little hitch, therefore we had to sleep at the train station in Osogbo. We were so happy the next day when we heard the loud and almost deafening sound of the train rolling into the station. When it finally halted, we made for the entrance where our tickets were checked as we boarded the train and took our seats.

It was very cosy inside the train and that made our journey very remarkable and exciting. We passed through Jebba, the River Niger, Kaduna, down to Kafanchan and finally, to Jos. The train station was packed full when we arrived because there was a lot of activities going on in the place. I kept wondering, when we arrived, if the whole town

was converged at the terminal. A delegation from the church was on hand to receive us and after we exchanged pleasantries, we were driven to the pastoral house where there were other people waiting to receive my family and I.

The pastoral house was a beautiful place, well-furnished and fitted with all that we needed. We left Igede with some of our personal belongings but we discovered we that we did not need them because all that we required had been provided for. The only thing we were not prepared for was the cold in Jos. The first few days were not too pleasant, especially for me, because I caught the flu and I was sneezing heavily. I tried as much as I could to brave the cold but I had a tough time containing it. My wife and children, however, adjusted quite well to the harsh weather. Because Jos was always so cold, the pastoral house was built mostly with planks to prevent much cold from getting in. Planks were used for the windows and furniture and that made the inside of the house very dark. We needed the lights on for 24 hours round the clock. On request, the church agreed that we could replace some of the window boards with glass. When that was done, everyone who visited marvelled at how beautiful and well-lit the house was.

While we were yet trying to settle down, I observed that Jos was quite a different place from Igede. For one, there were a lot of American Missionaries there but none in Igede. I noticed also, that attendance at church services was quite impressive on Sunday, sometimes numbering close to one thousand people. Weekly programmes, also recorded up to 500 people at prayer meetings on Mondays and Wednesdays. More interesting was the high number of Ogbomoso people and this made them to be recognized in Jos. Most of them were traders and they were very evangelistic.

After settling down fully, I began planning on how to build on the record of the church, both in attendance and evangelism. Later on, my sermons became offensive to some people and it caused attendance to reduce slightly. Concerned about the reason for low attendance, I asked around and I was shocked when I was told that some members of the church, especially some of the Ogbomosos, got offended by one of my sermons (I cannot remember which one ruffled them but I was sure I was telling the truth), and for that reason, they decided to stop attending services. That did not however deter me from preaching the truth, as I was sure that God was on my side, and even if they tried to do anything, they would only be trying to fall the wrong horse. Good for them, they could not confront me and they kept on with their lives.

Another altercation that I had was with some deacons, over the running of the Baptist Day School, one of the biggest schools in Jos. Long before my arrival in Jos, the two pastors who preceded me were engaged in a silent war with some deacons in the church because they (Deacons) did not want the pastors to be involved in the administration or affairs of the school. When I got to Jos and I tried to know what was going on in the school, my interest was rebuffed, and remembering what we were taught at the seminary to not interfere in church businesses, I decided to keep away, since I had my primary mission to face. I allowed them to keep running the school until they ran into troubled waters.

The deacons had been using the school finances to fund their businesses for a long time. One of them was in charge of the school finances which made it easy for them to borrow money at will for whatever purposes they needed it for. One of them ordered some goods from Lagos; unfortunately, the truck bringing the goods to Jos had an accident on the way and all the goods were destroyed. The news leaked but I pretended that I did not hear what happened. It was an open secret that the deacons were using the school's funds for their personal businesses but because of their clout, they could not be challenged. It went on like that until the unfortunate incident affected the finances of the school. It was, regrettably, a sad experience for them. Some people said I should have exposed their illicit act before the incident, but I did not think it was necessary, as I knew they would one day pay for their actions. They were disgraced and from that moment on, the church took control of the affairs of the school.

After the unfortunate incident, attendance at Sunday services improved, so did church offering. There was however a snag about the offering. It was always taken home by the treasurer, pending when it would be taken to the bank, because there was no suitable place to keep the money. I thought this was not safe and I called one of my friends, Deacon Ojewunmi who was working in a car dealership shop. I asked him where we could get a safe for the church and he directed me to a friend who was disposing off some safes. Immediately, I contacted the man and he told me the price, I rallied round and got money to buy the safe. The safe was sealed in a part of the wall of the church which made access to it very restricted Even the treasurer was psychologically relieved that he did not have to watch his back again. From then on, the offerings collected during the Sunday services were kept in the safe and on Monday morning, after the prayer meeting, the treasurer would come and count the money and take it to the bank.

Unlike Igede, the church in Jos had a car but before our arrival, it was sold, and the church decided it was not going to buy another one until much later. Nevertheless, the church provided me with a bicycle which I used whenever I had to go out. After a while, I saw that the church needed to expand, so I began searching for vacant plots of land in the town for the church expansion. Immediately I found an undeveloped piece of land, we contacted some people at the lands office to supply us with information on what the land was earmarked for. When we were told it was vacant, I rallied round and with the support of the missionaries, particularly Rev. Parham, we were able to secure the certificate of occupancy to take charge of the land. Rev. Parham was one of my good friends in Jos, he took to me quickly because we always seemed to agree on most issues. Though the land we bought was a little expensive, the church reasoned that it would be a wise decision if we acquired it. Since the land was extensive, the first thing we did was to build a primary school on one side of it. After its completion, many people agreed that it was one of the best primary schools built by any church in Jos. The plan for the school was drawn by experienced architects in the Mission and the best building materials were used. After a while, the Nassarawa Baptist Church was built on the remaining portion of the land and it too became a reference point for many people because of its sheer size and design. Once again, the good Lord had proved Himself worthy of praise.

The *Bowen University* Dream

The need to provide more scholarship to deserving and promising individuals was becoming increasingly urgent, therefore the Nigerian Baptist Convention and Southern Baptist Seminary in America decided to sponsor Rev. S.A. Lawoyin, Rev. E.O. Akingbala, Rev. E.O. Agboola, Dr. & Mrs. E.A. Dahunsi, Dr. & Mrs. Adegbite, Dr. E.L. Akinsanya, Rev. T.A. Adejumobi and some other people. After a while, it became financially tasking for the Convention to continue sending people on overseas scholarships, therefore, it was agreed that a Baptist University should be established in Nigeria. Immediately the idea received blessings, a committee was set up quickly to raise money for the project. I was still a pastor in Igede when my wife and I heard of the project and we began promoting it there. I made sure that I bought fund raising certificates for my wife and children. We also encouraged the members of the church to do the same. Upon our transfer to Jos, we continued to promote the scheme.

It was not long after we got to Jos that the Baptist Convention requested, through the church, that I joined in promoting the Baptist University dream. I had to be on loan to the Convention between June and December, 1961, to help raise money for the proposed Bowen University. Our task was to get a tenth of the total estimated initial cost of 40,000 pounds needed to build the Baptist University. The assignment took me all over the country, and to Ghana, where I created awareness, generated support and raised money. Chief J.O. Fagbemi was the chairman of the fund raising committee while Dr. (Mrs.) Adegbite was the treasurer. There were some other people on the committee also and we all showed commitment to the project. In Ghana, Rev. M.O. Olaleye and Rev. E.O. Oyekan assisted me to reach out to other fellow pastors to support this worthy cause. To make my job easy, the Convention bought a car for me which I used throughout the period I was away from Jos. Before I left for the assignment however, I planned a preaching schedule for the Deacons to use for the church while I was away.

I spoke at conferences, before associations and in Teachers' Colleges, to promote and raise funds for the university. I appealed to individuals and churches and to God be the glory, we received an overwhelming response. Donations were sent to the treasurer, Mrs. Adegbite, who issued certificate to donors. When the assignment was completed, we were able to raise over 40,000 pounds in cash and pledges. However, due to one reason or the other, the university could not take off at the time we anticipated but I thank God that today, the dream has crystallized into Bowen University, Iwo.

After the fund raising assignment was completed, the Convention wanted to sell off the car and asked if I wanted to buy it. Since I did not have enough money, I turned to the church to get a loan but the church told me that since I needed the car for the use of God's work, they would buy it. After the church bought the car, they offered me a driver but I objected, insisting that I wanted to drive myself because I knew that the deacons would want to use the car for their personal gains, which I would never support. The matter was eventually settled when one of my friends, Deacon Lawoyin intervened.

Grace gave birth to a girl during our stay in Jos. She was named Bunmi, but she died a few years later at the Plateau General Hospital, due to medical negligence after a brief illness. It was a trying period for us but with the help of the church, Dr. C.F. Whirley, Rev. E.O. Akingbola and Rev. J.A Olaniyan who supported us with prayers and words of comfort, we got over the shock. Despite the sad incident, we had a wonderful experience in Jos because of the things we were able to achieve through God's help and wisdom. We love the land and the people and when we look back, we always find reasons to thank God because not only did the membership of the churches in Jos and Plateau grow, we were also able to establish Baptist churches in Bauchi, Potiskum and Mubi provinces. I remember vividly that on one of my trips to Nassarawa where we were trying to establish a church, I was almost carried away in my car by flood because it rained heavily on that day. The flood was so heavy that it flushed the car to one side of the road. I became jittery and struggled with the car for minutes. At the point the flood started making its way into the car, I knew God had to intervene and He did. He saw me through that day.

JOS/ BUKURU – 1961 -1963

First Baptist Church, Jos 1961 – welcome service

Teaching at Bukuru

We enjoyed our stay in Jos and, in 1963, I decided it was time to move ahead and get better education abroad. My wife and I had the opportunity to be given mission scholarships for overseas duties and in August 1963, we bade farewell to Jos, to continue with my education in America.

First Baptist Church, Port-Harcourt: 1966

> *"Yea, though I walk through the valley of the shadow of death, I will fear no evil: for thou art with me; thy rod and thy staff they comfort me."*
>
> - *Psalm 23:4*

After our studies in America, we returned to Nigeria in 1966 and Port-Harcourt became our first place of assignment. At that time, there were speculations of an impending civil war in the country. Some people advised us against going to Port-Harcourt and that if we did, we should travel by train instead of going by road. My wife and I reunited with the children who had been staying with my sister in Ilorin while we were away and we set out for the journey. We travelled to Port-Harcourt from Oshogbo and it took us a longer time than usual to get to our destination because of the security operatives we came across in Jebba and Markudi, who stopped and searched commuters.

On getting to Port Harcourt, there were only a few people left to receive us at the train station. The others had left because of the late arrival of the train and there were no mobile phones then to inform our hosts of the train delays. Immediately we alighted from the train and completed all formal introductions, we were driven to the Mission house where we stayed for a couple of days before moving to our own apartment.

After two Sundays in Port-Harcourt, Governor Odimegwu Ojukwu gave a quit order to non-indigenes of the Eastern region to leave for their own region with immediate effect. A few days after that announcement, the palpable fear that had long gripped the hearts of many was finally confirmed. The civil war broke out. The danger signs were everywhere and by the time the people of Eastern origin began making their way home in droves, I knew that it was time for us who were from the West, to depart. The situation was further worsened when the corpses of Easterners killed in the North began arriving in the East for burial. Those who made it back alive either had some parts of their bodies severed or did not come back with any property or cash. When the Easterners saw what was done to their people, they began making reprisal attacks on the Northerners in the East. Looting took over and the whole town was thrown into chaos.

We were a little apprehensive of the situation and when the principal of Baptist High School, Chief A.B. Batubo, told us that he could not guarantee our safety any more, I knew our days were numbered. The principal made a quick arrangement for us to leave the city immediately, while the premises of the school filled up with easterners who were now being quartered in the school dormitory. The moment it dawned on me that it was unsafe to remain in Port-Harcourt, I dashed back home and told my wife what was happening. She was not so worried at first but I warned her to leave what she was doing, so that she would not turn to Lot's wife who refused to heed her husband's advice. When she sensed the seriousness in my voice, immediately she left what she was doing and began packing. At that moment, we remembered the children were in school and I quickly dashed out again to bring them home. When I saw Jaiye, he was looking for his sister. Fortunately, it did not take long before we found her. When we got home, my wife had packed the things she could and we had to leave some of our belongings with the principal who promised to take good care of everything. The cab drivers arrived a few minutes later and they helped us put our things in the back of the car. That done, the principal instructed two hefty men to protect us and make sure we got to Onitsha safely, which was the boundary between the Eastern and Western regions.

At Aba and Owerri, we saw a lot of soldiers on the road wielding guns and brandishing all sorts of weapons. When they stopped us at Aba, I alighted from the car and showed them my international passport. I explained to them that I was a pastor of the Baptist Convention and had just returned from overseas and did not know there was trouble in the country. After pleading with them, they allowed us to go. At Owerri, it was the same thing, the soldiers stopped us again and I gave them the same explanations I gave the soldiers in Aba. The drivers alternated with each other at intervals, stepping aside for the other when one was tired. Minutes after we left Aba, one of the drivers did something strange. He stopped the car, went into the bush and cut the branch of one tree. He took off the leaves and placed it in-between the mirrors outside the car. At my prodding, he explained to us that the branch was a symbol that we were not enemies of the Easterners.

As we descended the high hill leading to Onitsha, we saw armed and masked men jumping out from the bush. Immediately the drivers saw them, they knew there was trouble and they kept telling me to not step out of the car. All through, my wife and children were calm. When the car came to a halt eventually, the masked men started hitting it ferociously. Not satisfied, they surrounded it and started chanting in unified chorus that they wanted to eat flesh and drink blood. One of the drivers got out of the car quickly and shut the door swiftly. He stood by the door and began to speak heavily to them in Igbo language. From inside the car, we could sense the argument was hot though we could not understand what they were saying. After a few minutes of exchange of hot words by both men, we were allowed to move on. Sometime after that scary encounter, we arrived in Onitsha. It was a moment of respite for us. When the drivers parked properly and asked us to alight, I became a little worried because we were still in the Eastern territory. I begged them to take us to Benin since some of my in-laws lived there and they agreed to do so, only after I promised to pay them more money. We began the journey to Benin and with God's grace, we arrived Benin safely and, to the joy of my wife's family. We passed the night there but we could only leave for Igbara-Oke a few days later because the war had broken out there too. When we got to Igbara-Oke, our relations who had been worried and had been praying for our safety were very happy when they saw us. My father-in-law had set out to look for us and was waiting outside his house for a lorry that would take him to the East. However, Baba needed to use the toilet and whilst he went to ease himself, the vehicle had come and left, not waiting for him. God spared his life too. His travelling case was outside his house when we arrived.

The following day, I travelled to Ibadan to let the Convention know that my family and I had returned home safely. There were no telephones, whether landline or mobile, in those days. The entire Convention staff at the headquarters were happy when they saw me and we prayed to God to spare and preserve the lives of everyone involved in the work of God in the Baptist Mission, wherever they were.

Teacher/ Chaplain, Baptist High School, Saki: 1967
The rest of 1966 was spent in Igbara-Oke and Ogbomoso pending the time the Convention could post me to a new place; nevertheless, my wife

got teaching jobs in Ogbomoso and Igbara-Oke. Throughout the period of my waiting for my posting to another Church, the Convention continued to pay my salary. In January 1967, I was told that Saki Boy's High School required an English language teacher desperately, because the school needed the approval of the West African Examination Council (WAEC) to make the school an examination centre. According to the principal of the school, Deacon. S. L. Akinokun, they did not want their students going to Ibadan or elsewhere to sit for their examinations, so, I was contacted for the job. Since I was not doing anything, I took the job of teaching English language and Bible knowledge in the school. My efforts and that of the school were immediately fruitful. In no time, WAEC officials inspected the school and it was approved as an examination centre and this was joyful news for everyone. Sequel to that, many people began suggesting that since I could teach so well, I should be made the chaplain of the school. I accepted to serve and I gave a helping hand to the churches in Saki. Later that year, my wife gave birth to a boy at the Baptist Hospital under the supervision of Dr. Olu Fatunla. We named him Deji and his coming brought joy into our home. Later in 1967, I got a call to serve at Owu Baptist Church, Abeokuta, a familiar territory, as that was the same Church in which I was baptized. For that reason, I did not think long before I accepted the offer. When I notified the school authority that I wanted to leave, they were hesitant but I told them it was time for me to answer a bigger call. My service in Abeokuta began on January 1, 1968.

Pastor, Ago-Owu Baptist Church, Abeokuta: 1968-1969

Going to Abeokuta was like returning home and my wife did not object to our movement, since she could continue with her teaching profession in one of the schools. Fortunately for her, there was a school adjacent the church in Owu, so she did not need to look for another school to teach.

Owu Baptist Church was one of the biggest churches in Abeokuta. It served the staff and students of Premier Grammar School and Baptist Boys' High School, so, we were very honoured to go and serve there. My family was received by some Deacons and members of the church who welcomed us whole-heartedly. However, the church had problems with sitting space for members, and in order to overcome this challenge, a balcony, fully fitted with seats, was designed by Deacon Odebunmi, an architect, who doubled as the supervisor of the building project, together with Deacon Akinsanya and some members of the church.

There were other challenges we had to overcome. Two weeks after we got to Abeokuta, we lost our baby, Deji, who was barely a year old. Before then, Kemi had fallen ill and had to be hospitalized for days. On the day she was discharged from the hospital, we got home to find Deji had taken ill and was vomiting repeatedly. We rushed him to the Catholic Hospital but when we got there, the doctor was away on break. The nurse who attended to us administered an injection on him and since we could not wait for the doctor to return, as Deji's condition was worsening, we dashed to the General Hospital. When we got there, the doctor asked me to go home and get a water flask while my wife stayed back with our sick son. Unfortunately, the doctor did not take the full medical history of our son, what treatment he had received elsewhere, and my worried wife forgot to inform the doctor that Deji had been given an injection at the Catholic hospital prior to our arrival at the General Hospital. The doctor proceeded to give Deji another injection. My wife would tell me later that she felt life go out of our son immediately the injection was given, and that was how Deji died.

The loss was heart-breaking and it affected the entire family. Wondering, what was happening, some people started whispering in low tones that the incident was beyond the ordinary. One female member of the church even mouthed it loud that they had never witnessed such a thing before in the church. We had to seek solace and comfort in God, so that we could overcome the evil tide. We buried Deji with the help of Pa Abati, the father of Reuben Abati. He was one of our neighbours and it was in his backyard that our late son was buried. He supported us with words of comfort during that period. My wife was devastated by what happened, but as time went by, she got over it and we moved on. The loss of a child, at any age, can be devastating, and couples going through such a horrible experience will always need physical, emotional, and spiritual support, as well as prayers and this should not be ignored by the family and friends who are nearby.

The civil war was yet to abate when we got to Abeokuta, therefore, movement was heavily restricted and because of the nature of my assignment, which required that I move around town, I had to seek a way to move about freely. Fortunately for me, I heard that passes were being issued at the military adjutant's office and I went there to apply for one. I explained to the adjutant that I was the pastor of Owu Baptist Church and my work involved going out often on ministrations. After convincing him, he commanded the issuing officer to hand me a pass and I became the only pastor with a pass to move around Abeokuta. The pass was very helpful because day or night, I could move about without any hindrance. After a while, the soldiers deployed to Abeokuta to mount road blocks got acquainted with me and they always hailed me whenever I drove past in my car. I brought my 1600 model Volkswagen Beetle from Saki and it helped me a lot until the engine wore out some months later.

Subsequent to all the things that happened when we first arrived in Abeokuta, things began to change. We started a yearly revival in

Abeokuta and also created outside stations to cater to the needs of those who could not come to Owu. One of the stations we catered to was in Ewekoro which comprised a church and a school. The school and church later gave way to the Ewekoro Cement factory because it affected the physical growth of the church. The government, however, provided another place for us, where we then built a new school.

To the glory of God, attendance also improved in church and that raised the standard of giving to the work of the Lord. We took the issue of tithing seriously and we made sure that the parishioners never joked with their offerings and tithes. I preached about giving wherever we went and we made sure we impressed it on the people that, it was not just about giving but about working towards making God's salvation available to other souls. Giving good offerings to the Lord was one legacy we left behind in all the places we served and we always urged the congregation to continue with it. In 1969 our joy increased when my wife delivered another baby at the Catholic Hospital. This time, it was a girl and we christened her, Oluwaremilekun. Our joy knew no bounds when she was born because we believed that God had wiped away the tears of losing Deji with the birth of Oluwaremilekun.

In 1969, I was invited to the Convention to take up a position with greater responsibilities. In just two years of service in Abeokuta, we recorded quite a lot of positive achievements that when it was time to move, the members of the church did not want to let us go, as we had spent barely two years with them. The decision to leave was not mine. The Baptist Convention beckoned on me to take up the position of the Sunday School Secretary. It was beyond my powers or control to reject the call and remain in Abeokuta, and after due consultation, we decided to leave at the end of 1969.

CHAPTER SEVEN

ACROSS THE OCEANS

"Jesus said to them, 'Have you never read in the Scriptures: 'The stone which the builders rejected has become the chief cornerstone. This was the LORD's doing, and it is marvellous in our eyes'?
Matthew 21:42

The Journey to America
In 1963, I travelled to America on the bill of the Baptist Seminary to continue my education. My wife and I were given mission scholarships for overseas' duties, which meant that we could both enrol in any university abroad, with the financial support of the Convention. We were serving at First Baptist Church, Jos at this time. Before we travelled, a white couple, Mr. and Mrs. Harts came to Nigeria on holidays from America and they visited Jos. One Sunday morning, they asked somebody in the hotel they were lodging in, if there was any Baptist Church around where they could worship and they were directed to First Baptist Church, Jos.

When I saw them that Sunday morning in the service, I knew they were first time comers at the church and I welcomed them. During the announcement, I introduced those attending the service for the first time and I went ahead to introduce the Harts to the congregation too. After the service, I met them again and during our discussion, I told them that my wife and I would be going on scholarship to America. The news gladdened their hearts. They were from New York and most Baptist Churches were in the South, but they asked if my wife and I would not mind staying with them, first in New York, before I went off to school in North Carolina. I agreed to their request and when I travelled to America in 1963, I spent my first days in America in their home. It was a profitable introduction to life in America. They took me to so many places in town and I really enjoyed my stay with them.

One unforgettable experience I had while I was staying with them was when I was asked if I needed anything to eat. I was asked just once and it was never repeated. At the moment when I was asked, I was alright. I expected to be asked again, but, they never did. This was unlike Nigeria where you are asked a million and one times if you needed something to eat. I became very hungry and I could not call anyone since I had told them that I was not hungry. I managed to cope with nothing in my stomach until the following day. The next day when I was asked if I needed anything to eat, I quickly told them 'yes', and, what I wanted. That was my very first lesson. The couple also took me to their club house and some other places so I could have a feel of America. They always introduced me as a big Pastor from Nigeria because the congregation size of First Baptist Church, Jos was quite large. At prayer meetings, we recorded close to 500 people in attendance, even with the fact that Jos was very cold!

The Harts were very kind and generous to me. They bought me a suit and gave me some other things when I was leaving for school. They did not, however, stop at that. Throughout my stay in America, they kept on sending money to me at Christmas to send to my wife and children. It became certain that my family would receive something from Mr. and Mrs. Harts every Christmas and when I left for Wake Forest, they made sure that I had a safe transit.

Arrival at Wake Forest: My Tail Story

When I arrived at Wake Forest University[4], North Carolina, I was accommodated in the home of another couple. The Elkins were retired and their son had served as a Peace Corps member in Nigeria. They were very accommodating and good to me. Staying with them was full of mixed memories. The Elkins had a little daughter who, whenever I took my bath, took a peep at me. She did that for a couple of times, then one day, I heard her whispering her discovery to Mrs. Elkins; "He has no tail! He has no tail". I cannot remember what Mrs. Elkins said but she seemed to have quieted the child momentarily. Her curiosity not satisfied, she came peeping again on another day. On that occasion, I asked her to come closer and wondering what I wanted to do, she obliged. I showed her my bare back. She was uncomfortable but surprised. I told her that I was not a monkey as she had been made to believe. She went back to Mrs. Elkins and told her again that I had no tail. They had lived with the impression that people from Africa were monkeys who lived on trees and had long tails dangling behind their backs. Most of the things they knew about Africa, as I later got to know, were shown to them at the cinemas. They were shown gorillas and were told that Africans were senior gorillas. That day, I went further to ask her if I was different from her dad. She stood there dismayed. I did not feel bad about her action. She was just a child who could not control herself because of what she had been made

---

4   www.wfu.edu

to believe. I knew that she was not going to report her latest discovery to Mrs. Elkins alone, but would also report to her classmates at school that the African man living with them had no tail. The Elkins never said anything about the issue. They kept sealed lips throughout my stay with them and I never bothered to bring the matter up as well.

Segregation in Wake Forest

My first days at Wake Forest University were full of many experiences. I was the second African to study in the University. I got to know about the university through one of the American missionaries in Nigeria. He sent his daughter, Diana, to the school because many missionaries did not like the segregation in America at that time, having been to different parts of the world. They were one of those who believed that anyone from anywhere, as long as they were qualified, should be able to study anywhere. Diana studied at Wake Forest University and it was when she was there that they stopped segregation. The students spear-headed the historic campaign for the abrogation of segregation which meant that Africans could now study at Wake Forest University.

Prior to the abrogation of the policy, the first African-applicant was from Ghana, unfortunately he was not allowed to stay because segregation was still rife in the school. He had to go to a Negro College in Wake Forest before he was allowed, later, to go back to the university. Later, when things were put right, people, especially from Africa, now had unfettered access to study at the school. By the time I got to Wake Forest, things had been regularized and I became the first African who started and finished in the school without any interruption.

The President of the school, Dr. H. Trible was a very good man. He was so kind to me that every time he saw me on the campus, though we had thousands of students in the university, he would stop and ask if I was in contact with my family and the Convention in Nigeria. He would ask if the weather was good for me and how I was coping with my studies. He made my life very pleasurable. There was another professor who was very kind to me. He had been to Nigeria many times. He was a good friend of Sir Francis Ibiam and Dr. J.T. Ayorinde, so he knew much about Nigeria and the people. The professor invited me to his house all the time but I was not comfortable with going there because it was always cold. There was a day I went there and had to run back. He never warmed his house except when he was at home. Once he was out, he simply removed the wood from the furnace. He did all he could to persuade me to visit his house more frequently but I could not contain the cold.

Away Alone

My wife could not come with me to America in 1963 because although she had obtained a Grade III teacher training certificate in Domestic Science and Home Economics at Ilesa Government College, to qualify to be in a university in America, she needed a Grade II Teacher's certificate. She attended Methodist Teachers College, Sagamu, and obtained her Grade II certificate. I wanted to travel early because three of my classmates had left before me. My wife was jittery at first, but, since she was coming to join me very soon, her fears were soon erased. At first, it was the children's welfare that gave us concern but God so good, my sister, Sarah, said she would help us take care of the children when my wife would have joined me in America. All the while I was alone, I missed her a great deal and always looked forward to the day she would join me. When she finally did, sometime in 1965, she enrolled to study at the university and we both stayed in the couple's quarters in the school. She studied for a diploma in religious education at the seminary, because she could not stay to finish a degree programme.

Education in America

Studying in America was not an easy task, you were expected to know everything. The subjects we studied were very unlike what obtained in Nigerian Universities. It, however, became an advantage to me later because I was able to have sufficient knowledge on a number of issues. American education is broad, particularly if you are studying for the first degree but it is much relaxed at the Master's Degree level.

Though America had the best educational facilities, we made the decision then that we would not allow any of our children to study abroad at undergraduate level because we felt it was better if they studied in Nigeria first and could, later, proceed abroad for higher degrees. We had opportunities to bring them to America while I was there alone and, even when my wife joined me, but we felt it was not the best thing to do because we studied the lifestyle in America and concluded that it would not be beneficial to them. Before my wife joined me, I kept in constant touch with her and the children by writing letters to them and to which they, also, always responded promptly.

One interesting thing about America is that no matter how remote a place is, there were social infrastructures like electricity, water and good roads. Letters could get anywhere as long as your mail box was in front of your house. Most of what you had in cities, you would always get in the suburbs. I always wished we could have things like that in Nigeria.

The Rejected Stone

I had thought that all the churches in America were liberal and there was no discrimination among denominations but I was subjected to racial segregation. One memorable incident occurred when I wanted to become a member of a Baptist Church in Louisville, Kentucky, but I was rejected because I was a black man. The first Sunday that I attended the church, the presiding pastor stood by the door after the service to shake hands with parishioners as they filed out. He shook hands with those who filed before me, who were white, but when it got to my turn, I noticed that his attitude changed. Instead of shaking my hands, he simply ignored me. It continued like that for a couple of weeks. I would wait a while for him to shake my hand but he never did. One Sunday, he announced in church that those who were interested in becoming members of the church among the visitors should stand up for recognition and admittance. I stood up and so did other new members. I was the only African. The names of those who stood up were announced to the congregation and the congregation was asked if it wanted to accept the new members into their fold. They all shouted "Yes", if they wanted. When it got to my turn, the pastor overlooked me. It was as if I was not standing there physically. I was shocked and my mind kept wondering why I was being treated like an outcast, particularly in the house of God, which should know no race or colour.

The pastor went ahead to call names of the other persons. When I was almost convinced in my heart that I was not wanted, he suddenly turned his sight on me and said what I could not readily comprehend. He announced that I should see him after the service. I did as I was told. When I met him after the service, what he told me was astonishing. He said it was beyond him to accept me because I was black and it could lead to the loss of some members of the church who did not favour people like me attending their church, especially since I was from Africa. It was as if I was dreaming. I went home that day feeling and looking dejected.

Coincidentally, the pastor's sister was a missionary in Nigeria and we were friends in our church in Ago-Owu. She made them aware that there was going to be trouble if it was reported back in Nigeria that I had been refused admittance by a Baptist Church in America. Dr. Patterson, my principal in B.B.H.S. Abeokuta, thankfully, was on leave to America with his wife during this trying period. They waded into the matter and informed the pastor that I was not a *small man* in Nigeria. They told him that I had been the recording secretary of the Nigeria Baptist Convention for years and I had served in some of the biggest churches in the country. Dr. Patterson advised that something be done immediately. That same week, the pastor apologized and begged me to come to church the following Sunday. There was little or nothing I could say as I accepted his apology. When I got to church the next Sunday, the pastor informed the congregation that they had to accept me because I was somebody to be reckoned with in the Baptist seminary.

During the service that Sunday, the congregation voted unanimously that I could become a member of the church. I was immediately admitted and it became big news all over the town. It was broadcast on radio and television that Highland Baptist Church had just accepted the first African as a member. It was a moment of joy and triumph for me. It made me proud to be an African man. Ironically, one of my professors, Jester, was on mission in Nigeria and was sponsored by that same church, yet they could not readily accept me as one of their own!

After my admittance, I knew I had just won a big victory. Later, the Baptist Mission Secretary for Africa invited me to lunch and during our discussion he said: "You are to regard yourself as a missionary to some of our people here." He said many of the whites only gave out money to support the missions abroad but did not know much about the people. He added that he would henceforth make Americans realize that as much as they could travel to other countries, so could other nationals come to America and be a part of the Baptist Convention.

I did not feel bad about being rejected because it was a known thing all over the world that blacks were being humiliated in America at the time. I thank God for the way He helped me to overcome that obstacle. Good enough, I was able to meet great people who were very good to me.

Friends along the Way
In the course of the week that I was accepted as a member of the church, one of the members, Mr. Alwes came to visit me at home. He apologized on behalf of the church for the way I was treated. As for me, I had nothing against anybody, but only wondered why the church would send missionaries to Africa to open our eyes to the word of God and still see us as second-class citizens of the world. Mr. Alwes and I became friends and we developed a very good relationship from then on. He was a Sign Writer who made signboards and was always willing to listen to me and share with me whatever he had. During the course of our friendship, he got to know that I did not have a car. Meanwhile, he had a 1959 Chevrolet, a very big car that he was not driving. He serviced the car and gave it to me as a show of his kindness. I was surprised by his kind gesture. I used the car for the remaining part of my stay in America. Mr. Alwes later paid a firm in Italy to ship a car to Nigeria for me, but, it was not delivered. Long after I finished at the University and during one of my trips, I visited Rome twice, to know what was happening to the car. It was on one of my trips from Sweden that I stopped by for the second time at the firm and I learnt that the firm had gone bankrupt and had stopped shipment of cars.

Hogle Alfred was another good friend that I met in America. He was my classmate and it did not take long before we bonded as friends. I had his assistance anytime I needed it. He was not a racist and did not see anything wrong with the fact that I was an African. The two of us did most things together and it helped me a great deal. At school, we were required to type all our term papers and assignments. Some students who had their wives with them at the university and, who could type, did the job. Some collected money while others did not. Hogle knew that I could type and he had a typewriter which he could not use very well, so he gave it to me. He was very good and kind. He took me to several places and rendered lots of assistance to me.

The Death That Shook Me
Rev. Gilliland was one of the very good professors we had at the seminary back in Nigeria. He died a few months after I got to America. He was a very down to earth person. He was in charge of the electrical facilities at the seminary and he also serviced the cars of his fellow missionaries. He was under a car while repairing it, when the car lost its balance and hit him on the head. They could neither treat him in the seminary hospital nor in Lagos, so he was flown to America. When I heard about the accident while in North Carolina, I wrote to let him know that I had heard about the unfortunate incident. The letter was apt and contained just a line; "Rev. Gilliland, I sympathize with you, *Olorun a wo e san o* (God will heal you)." It was his wife who took the letter to the hospital and read it to him. When she read the English part of it, I learnt that he only stared but when he heard the part I wrote in Yoruba language, it was as if something came into him. I was told that he woke up immediately and that he seemed happy.

Mrs. Gilliland then wrote me to ask that whenever I needed to write, I should do so in Yoruba language. From then, I began corresponding with them in Yoruba language until one day, when the President of the seminary called me to inform me of the sad news that Rev. Gilliland was dead. I was so pained by the news that tears ran down from my eyes. The President of the school told me later that the wife and family of Rev. Gilliland requested that I came to represent Nigeria at his burial in Alabama. This was at the height of segregation in America, especially in Alabama, so I was advised by Rev. Gilliland's wife to dress in Nigerian attires, so that I would not be mistaken for those who were causing trouble. Since I did not have a sizable number of western attire; that was not a problem.

I was lodged in a beautiful hotel and on the day of the burial, I was called upon to give a short testimony on Rev. Gilliland. When I stood up to talk, tears lurked in the corner of my eyes but I held it in. My speech was short and I seized the opportunity to not only extol the virtues which he lived for, but to share with those who attended the burial, his good services to Nigeria while he was with us. As one of his old students, I said all I knew about him, especially how useful he was in Nigeria. He was buried in his village later that day and it was a sad day for those of us who knew him.

Challenges of a Foreign Student
At Wake Forest, nothing was free; you had to work for it. Studies were hard, particularly for us who were foreigners, who did not have a background in certain areas. For instance, if we had prior information that we would be dissecting frogs in the biology class, most of my classmates had dissecting sets in their homes and they would have practiced ahead of the class, unlike the rest of us who did not have the sets and did not have the same opportunity. Most of the American students had binoculars and other science equipment at home, while I was still asking for the names of instruments and how they were used!

They had many books that could help them to understand what we were being taught. If they could not get the required books in the library, their parents got it for them. Although they were better equipped for a lot of the lessons, most of them were laid back and always put off their assignments until a later time. Since I did not have that luxury, I seized the opportunity to do my assignments by making use of the instruments I loaned or borrowed from some of them. It helped me tremendously and I scored higher marks in class.

Opportunity to Make Money

In all American schools, there was always an opportunity to make money and when one came my way, I did not allow it to pass by me. Buoyed by the experience I had while I worked as a librarian in B.B.H.S, I asked if I could get something similar in America. The operation was a little different though. Students would bring a list of the books they needed and I would pick it for them. When they finished reading, they left the books on the table whenever they were leaving. There was a full-time paid staff librarian while working students like me worked for a couple of hours, signed for those hours and left to do other things.

After I got my Bachelor of Arts degree in Theology at Wake Forest, immediately I went ahead to obtain a Bachelor's degree in Divinity also. This time at the seminary, we had to study Hebrew and Greek in order to graduate because the original Bibles were written in the two languages. The Old Testament was written in Hebrew while the New Testament was written in Greek.

While studying for my second bachelor's degree, I applied for a job in the library again but, this time, the quota for students was filled except I was interested in becoming a book binder. I said I did not have the knowledge of book binding but I was told that I would be taught. In no time, I was able to soak up the knowledge. When I was learning, I was also being paid for the hours that I put in. The good thing about working as a book binder was that whenever you completed a job, you had to put your name on the book. This was necessary for two reasons; to know who did it in case of any complaint, and, for historical purposes. A lot of Nigerians who have visited Wake Forest have seen some of the books I worked on. We were taught in America to be self-reliant. You did not need to call a carpenter to fix any minor repairs in your home. You also did not need the electrician or plumber for anything. I learnt to fix many faults myself.

Interest in Radio and Television
While I was studying, I developed an interest in radio and television broadcasting when I saw the role both could play in spreading the gospel. We were doing something on radio in Ibadan, Kaduna, and Port-Harcourt in Nigeria, and a few other places, but we lacked adequate human resources. There were no trained Africans in broadcasting; it was the missionaries who did most of it. Upon graduation in June, 1966, I told the Mission in Nigeria that I wanted to stay back to take a course in radio and television at, Texas. The mission gave me the go-ahead to take the course as long as it would enrich the work of the Baptist Convention in Nigeria. Southern Baptist Convention in America had a radio and television commission in Texas, and they were the ones who arranged for me to go to Fort Worth. At Fort Worth, I had the opportunity of seeing where former American president, J.F Kennedy was murdered. I was not the only one who was interested in the course; there were two other people from different missions who had been doing full time radio and television work in their different countries. I had a wonderful experience

*Doctor of Ministry, Southern Baptist Theological Seminary.
Louisville, Kentucky May 1974.*

there and I looked forward to the day when I would be able to put to practice, all the things I had learnt in the school.

Whilst at Forthworth and, on a cold day, Grace and I decided to go shopping for some groceries. We were walking to the shops when suddenly, we were stopped by the Police and interrogated. We were taken to their station in a car about four miles away. We had nothing to hide and after all their long questioning and checks, they were satisfied and said we could go and with no apologies, they refused to take us back to the spot where we were stopped in the first instance.. We had to trek back in the cold. It was another experience of discrimination and injustice that I faced, this time along with my wife, in the United States of America.

After obtaining my certificate, my resolve was to return to Nigeria and allow others to handle the church while I went into religious broadcasting, but, as God would have it, it was a different challenge that I faced when I returned home. The Convention said they were not ready to release me to go into religious broadcasting as my experience was needed more in developing the church. Not long after, in 1966, First Baptist Church, Port-Harcourt invited me to pastor the church, just about the time the civil war began.

Journey to Canada and Jerusalem

I went to Canada in 1980, for the Baptist World Alliance (BWA) meeting. By coincidence, the conference was going to be at the same period of the Holy Pilgrimage to Israel. Prior to my visit to the Holy Land, I always thought Bethlehem, Jerusalem, Canaan and other places that we read about in the Holy Bible no longer existed on the earth. The first person I knew who visited Jerusalem was an Anglican clergyman, Rev. T.A.J.

Ogunbiyi who visited the Holy Land in 1944 and who, on his return, regaled us with different stories of all that he saw. From that time, I looked forward to the day that I would be in Jerusalem to feel the awesomeness of God. Whilst I was studying in the United States of America, some of my classmates who had gone to the Holy Land told me about the places, but since I could not finance the trip when I was in the university, I had to wait until I was prepared to embark on the journey.

My dream to visit the Holy Land eventually came true in 1980. I had saved enough money, and I thought of combining my first Holy pilgrimage with the congress trip to Canada. The Convention was going to pay for my trip to Canada. What I needed to do was pay for my trip to Jerusalem. The treasurer told me the difference and I paid it. I went to Toronto, Canada and immediately the conference was over, I headed for Jerusalem. Before leaving Nigeria, I got a few people who wanted to go on the pilgrimage as well. My sister Sarah and five other people said they were interested in going also.

Jerusalem was so real and so amazing. It meant so much to every one of us who went on the trip such that we decided that we would henceforth plan to visit Jerusalem every year, during our holidays. We also agreed that we would help more people to go for the Holy pilgrimage. After I returned from the first trip to Jerusalem, I set out to work on how to get more people on the programme, to enjoy that experience of a lifetime. I could not, however, embark on the trip in 1982 and 1983 due to some ill health.

The Return to the Holy Land
In 1984, I was able to go on my second trip to Jerusalem which I had so much looked forward to with excitement. This time, I took many

people on the trip. I did not restrict myself to Baptists; I took Catholics, Anglicans and other people who were interested in making the trip. My second trip was very pleasant. We had devotions every morning as we were led by God. We stayed in hotels in Jerusalem and Tiberias. Things were made easy because some of the people who went with me this time were grounded in religious work and they assisted me in executing all that we needed to do. At every historical site, I would open my Bible to the passage where things concerning the site was written. For example, the place where Jesus Christ ascended into heaven was one of the places we visited. Till today, the foot prints of Jesus are ingrained on the ground, looking very fresh, still. The place is a sacred site for travellers or visitors to the Holy Land and it is preserved for one to have communion with God. The sacred site gives you the opportunity to decide that from the moment you visit the site, you would walk as Jesus walked. Once you said the prayer, you are to trust that God would assist you from that moment onwards, to always walk in His way. After the prayer, we then placed our feet in the footprints of Jesus.

One interesting and significant thing about this, is that everybody's feet matched the foot prints of Jesus perfectly. Whether you had big or small feet, they just fit perfectly. It was a wonderful experience. It was an extraordinary moment for me and that feeling has continued to live with me till today.

Another site that we visited was a church in Jerusalem called *The Church of all nations*. Inside the church, the Lord's Prayer is written in different languages that are spoken all over the world. The first time I visited the Church, there were just 26 languages displayed on the walls. Unfortunately, there was no Nigerian language. It was very surprising to us that, as big as Nigeria was, we were not represented. I hope that in future, we would have the prayer clearly and proudly written in Yoruba, Igbo and Hausa languages, for the world to see.

Another interesting place we visited was the home of Jesus Christ. The house is a three-storey building and people live on the ground floor. The carpentry shed where Joseph, the father of Jesus Christ worked, is still very intact, well-preserved and well-maintained. The *St. Joseph Church* is on the last floor of the building. Not only do you see these things, you feel them, and that feeling will remain with you forever, and your life will be transformed, definitely! We visited River Jordan afterwards and it became another life-transforming site for me. Everybody on the trip who wanted to, had a fresh baptism. Some of those who had been baptized before in Nigeria said they still wanted to be baptized by immersion in the River Jordan. Not only did I baptize them, I baptized myself too! The visit revealed the Bible to me in a comprehensible manner. That experience made me decide that I will serve God forever, without looking back. In all, I led about 100 pilgrims from different denominations, and four of my family members to Israel in 1980, 1981, 1984 and 1985. It was a worthwhile experience!

CHAPTER EIGHT

CALL TO HIGHER DUTIES

"Brethren, I do not count myself to have apprehended; but one thing I do, forgetting those things which are behind and reaching forward to those things which are ahead, I press toward the goal for the prize of the upward call of God in Christ Jesus."

Philippians 3:13-14

I was baptized in First Baptist Church; Ago-Owu, Abeokuta, in 1946 by Dr. Ayorinde and it was a joy to me when I was informed that my services were needed in the church years after. Apart from the personal fulfilment that I would have in serving the people, Abeokuta was like a second home to me. I accepted the call to serve in Abeokuta and in just two years of our stay, there was a marked improvement in attendance, membership, offering and tithing. We were to carry on with the work when a call came in 1969 that I was needed to serve in a higher position at the Nigerian Baptist Convention in Ibadan. A vacuum had been created by the retirement of Miss Ethel Hammon, the secretary of the Sunday school who was going on furlough, preparatory to her retirement.

She had been in charge of the Sunday School Secretariat for 32 years, from 1938 to 1970. The Convention knew that she would leave someday and they had groomed someone who would take over from her when she finally departed. One of my friends, and a strong member of the Convention, Rev. D.O. Idowu had worked for many years with her and he was seen as her undisputed successor. He was given the necessary training and sent on courses both within and outside Nigeria to enable to him take full charge. There was no formal announcement, but to say that he was next in line would be stating the obvious because Rev. Idowu was now fully knowledgeable in the administration of the Sunday school. He was honest and upright, he loved the work very much and everybody looked forward to the day when a Nigerian would take absolute control of the Sunday school work.

Few months before the final departure of Miss. Hammon, a shocking and unexpected incident shook the entire Baptist Convention. Rev. Idowu had gone on an official assignment to Oyo and was returning to Ibadan when he had a fatal motor accident. We were told that he drove himself and died on the spot while the person who sat next to him in the car survived the crash. His death was a massive blow to everybody in the Convention. It shook us like the force of a train and we were all tossed into mourning. Rev. Idowu was someone that we all loved but, beyond that, the post that was being reserved for him was going to become vacant.

The Sunday School Challenge
The Convention was almost brought to a standstill because of the two situations at hand. Miss Hammon could not be stopped from leaving Nigeria and the person who was supposed to take over from her had just died in a car crash. The Convention needed to act swiftly because

the work had to go on, thus a search began for the person who would fill the vacuum but it was a big task for the Convention because nobody else was positioned to take over. Meanwhile, my family and I were having a good time in Abeokuta. We were beginning to break new grounds because the church was serving the principals and members of staff of Premier Grammar School and Baptist Boy's High School, as well as the congregation.

A few weeks after the death of Rev. Idowu, the Convention met and decided that there was somebody who could do the job. The lot fell on me. I did not know what was going on then, but later, I received a notice that some delegates were coming down to Abeokuta to see me. I never for once predetermined the purpose for their coming. The delegation arrived and we had a lengthy discussion during which I was reminded about the unfortunate incident of Rev. Idowu and the retirement of Miss Hammon. In the course of our discussion, the delegation dropped the news that the Convention had reached a consensus that I should take up the duty of the Sunday school secretary.

I was stunned by the news. It was a big challenge and I could not give an immediate reply. When I finally found my voice, I told the delegation that the decision to heed or to not heed the call would be tough to take independently. More importantly, the work in Abeokuta was taking a huge and beautiful shape and we were hoping to complete what we had set out to do. That much I told the Convention delegates but they were not impressed with my stand but continued to stress the reasons why I should take up the appointment. Since I could not act alone, I directed them to the church. I needed also, to consult with my wife, because in every decision I had to make, I made sure that I put her and the children in the picture. The delegation went ahead to meet some members of the church and for days they had marathon meetings. To their bewilderment, the church told them they were not ready to let me go because I had barely spent two years in the church and they wanted me to stay and finish the work we had started. It became an arduous task for the delegation to convince the church. They pressed further for my release by telling the church in Abeokuta that although their church was an important part of the Convention, I was needed at this point in time, to serve the entire Baptist Convention in a higher capacity.

To Be or Not To Be
After a series of consultations and meetings, the delegation succeeded in convincing the church, who then decided that they were leaving the final decision to go or stay, to me. I was, thus, caught between staying in Abeokuta and leaving to take up the more challenging appointment. I could still not make up my mind immediately.

I had a mentor in Abeokuta, Rev. Agboola, the Pastor of Ijaiye Baptist Church, the first Baptist church in Abeokuta. In addition, he was once the Pastor-in-charge of First Baptist Church, Jos, long before I served there. He was to me, a father in the Lord, and I had great respect for him. I called him and explained the two options I was faced with. Not unexpectedly, he told me that I did not have any other choice than to leave Abeokuta to take up the bigger appointment. When I expressed my fears to him, he promised to give his support and give me whatever I needed to succeed in the task ahead. I also sought the advice of Deacon Akinsanya who was like a father to me and was my teacher at B.B.H.S. Abeokuta. When I consulted him, he, as well, was in support of me leaving for Ibadan. He told me that I should not be fearful but, rather, I should allow the will of God to be done. My wife wanted me to go, saying that she was willing to stand by me in whatever I decided to do. On my part, I sought God through prayers for divine intervention and allowed Him to take pre-eminence over the matter. The will of God was done, and eventually, I accepted the appointment and resumed as the Sunday School Secretary on January 1, 1970.

Daily Bible Reading with Notes

Immediately I assumed the post, one of the responsibilities I was saddled with was continuing from where Miss Hammon stopped. Thankfully, I had capable people on ground to work with: Mrs. Kehinde Opadoyin and Deacon Emman Oketokun were of great help. They were honest and hardworking people and they made my job very simple. There were also field workers for the North, the Mid-west and the West. Rev. Bako Sidi, Rev. Gbemi Otolorin, Rev. Mbasirike, Rev. Kayode, Rev. Egbonoje, Rev. Lateju and Rev. Ojedokun were some of the people God used to assist me in the task. The job of the Sunday School Secretary was enormous. You worked for the whole Convention and for you to succeed in that role, God had to be with you. I sought prayers from many Christian friends because I could not do the job alone. Sunday school had taken such a gigantic step in the promotion of God's work in the Baptist Convention that no one could afford to toy with it. One of the other big tasks I had was to produce locally, the Baptist literature that had previously been imported from America.

I discovered that many people needed additional explanations for the passages if they were to really appreciate the literature. I thought and prayed about this and in 1972, I sat down and developed the *Daily Bible Reading with Notes*. Writing the literature took a lot of time, a whole year precisely. When the first edition came out, the Convention was flooded with commendation letters. One of the greatest successes of the devotional book was that it was not only the Baptist Convention that made use of it, other denominations also embraced it. It was written in a way that everybody could understand. I thank God for that aspect of the work because it grew to the extent that the Baptist Convention in Nigeria was beginning to be called the Baptist Convention for Africa. We thank God for all the things the team and I were able to achieve. To Him be the glory!

Sunday School Anniversary
1979 marked the 125th year of Sunday school work in Nigeria. I felt it would be unwise if we waited till the 150th or 200th anniversary before we did anything, for two reasons. First, 125 years was no mean feat and secondly many people may not be around to celebrate the 150th year. I was encouraged by the support I got from everybody when I told them about the need to celebrate, and after we all agreed, a committee was set up to see to the success of the anniversary. A list of guests was drawn and one person whose name was prominent on it was Miss Hammon, who had long retired and had gone back to America. As the first Permanent Sunday School Secretary to promote what began in 1854, her presence was highly compulsory. Expectations were high, considering the fact that I was the first African to hold the post of the Sunday School Secretary. We needed to prove to the Southern Baptist Mission in America that though we are Africans, we could act brilliantly in any position, if given the opportunity. We lined up so many activities to celebrate the anniversary and all the people that we invited turned up to celebrate with us.

Miss Hammon arrived a few days before the ceremony and she was impressed, not only with the level of preparation, but by what we had been able to achieve in those years after her retirement. A delegation from the Southern Baptist Mission, USA, the Olubadan of Ibadan, top government functionaries, representatives of the Christian Association of Nigeria and people from other denominations were in attendance. It was a grand celebration.

Later that day, a plaque was dedicated to Miss Hammon and Rev. and Mrs. Bowen at Old Ijaiye, the place where Sunday school work began in 1854. Baptist Missionary work actually began in Ijaiye, Abeokuta in 1850 when Rev. Bowen came to Nigeria. For three years, he did the work alone until 1954 when he went to America on furlough and returned to Nigeria with his wife. She laid the foundation for Sunday school work in the Baptist Mission in their home, starting with their gardener and a few other people in 1854. A dinner party was held at the Government House in Ibadan during which I received a special Bible gift from the Southern Baptist Mission for what we were able to achieve. It was a great moment for my wife and I, and for the children also, who were all around to celebrate with us.

Before my retirement as the Sunday School Secretary, I also assisted the Baptist Association of Ibadan in all its activities. The association met four times a year to seek ways of expanding the Baptist church in Ibadan. In appreciation of my service as the Sunday School Secretary they made me the adviser of the body. I made sure that I attended all their meetings and I worked with so many individuals, particularly, Dr. Ayorinde, Dr. Dahunsi and Dr. Akande who were the General Secretaries of the association in the years that I served as the adviser. I gave leadership and service to the association where and when required, until I retired in 1986.

Baptist World Alliance Meetings
While serving as the Sunday School Secretary, I had the opportunity of representing the Convention at the annual Baptist World Alliance

meetings held to discuss how to improve Baptist work all over the world. The first meeting of the alliance that I attended was in Miami, Florida, in 1965. I was a student in America at that time and I joined the delegation from Nigeria at the meeting. In one of the subsequent meetings, I had the chance or opportunity of delivering a paper to the youths of the Baptist Convention. It was a rare opportunity for me and significantly, William Tolbert, an African, was elected as the President of the Baptist World Alliance at that meeting. The election of an African was received with a resounding applause, especially in Africa. Tolbert held the position for five years and he acted impressively. I attended three meetings after then and I also attended the 2005 meeting in Birmingham, England as one of the delegates. It would be 100 years since the meeting was first held in London in 1905.

In 1983, I had the honour of addressing delegates to the Alabama Baptist Convention in America. As part of its expansion and foreign missions programme, the Alabama Baptist Convention looked towards the direction of Nigeria for a programme on evangelism. The programme was aimed at strengthening the hold of the Baptist Convention in the areas where it was established. I was made the assistant co-coordinator of the programme and my duty was to make sure that evangelism work spread to every nook and cranny of Nigeria. My team and I tried our best to make sure that the task was achieved and at the end of the programme, I was invited to America to give a full report of what we had accomplished with the alliance.

I was also a member in one of the commissions of the Baptist World Alliance and one of the concerns of the commission was towards developing the Sunday school. The Sunday school is regarded as an important educational arm of the Baptist Convention and nothing was spared to make sure it remained so. The commission I served in was mandated to plan programmes that will enhance religious education in Baptist Conventions all across the world. In doing that, some of us in the commission travelled to Singapore to see what we could benefit from their educational system. The visit was an eye-opener and the knowledge that I brought back from the trip helped me to appreciate the roles leadership has to play in a developing nation like Nigeria.

Leaders Are Givers
Different people have different definitions of who a leader is. For me, a leader must be a good shepherd. He must lead by example and must be honest in all his dealings. My travels across some developed countries of the world have revealed so many things to me that when you have received so much from God and the people, you should in turn give back to those who need your help or assistance. In my case, I received so much from many people and it is only right that I assist those who are less fortunate. Giving is one quality that a good leader must possess. It is one big lesson that I learnt and I have tried as much as possible to teach it and live it. We are all debtors and since we cannot pay our debts to God directly, we should pay it to those in need!

One of the people who influenced me a great deal was William Carey. He was a roving preacher who went on modern missions to different countries on his own. He was a shoemaker and he gave up shoemaking to start working with indigenous people in India. He was there until he died on the mission field and one of his philosophies concerning leadership was that God should be first in everything we do, family second and self, last.

My Other Service Years

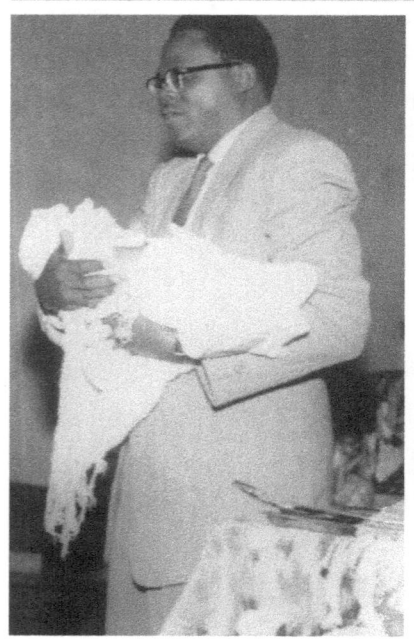

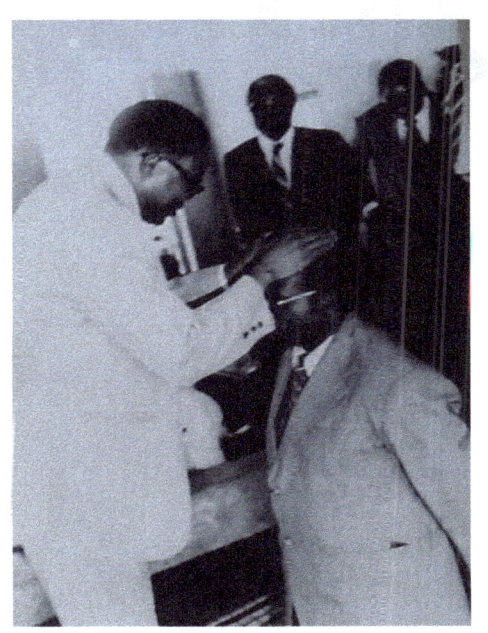

CHAPTER NINE

RETIRED BUT NOT TIRED!

"You did not choose me, but I chose you and appointed you to go and bear fruit - fruit that will last..."

John 15:16

After over three decades of service to the Convention, I knew it was time to leave. Following due consultations with my family, I gave the Baptist Convention notice that I wanted to retire. Expectedly, the Convention did not want me to leave and so it was with many people. All attempts to make me stay on in the various positions I was serving were unsuccessful because I was sure it was time to bow out and give other people a chance. When the Convention saw that I could not be convinced to stay on, it had no other choice than to accept my retirement.

My years of service to the Convention were counted from the day and year I got admitted to the seminary in 1952, to the day that I decided to retire. The Convention felt that I had put in enough hard work in the advancement of God's work and I needed to be rewarded. A befitting send-off party was organized for me and invitation cards were sent out to all the conferences that made up the Baptist Convention. So many other people were also invited. The send-off service was held at the Bodija Estate Baptist Church, Ibadan. Many people including the wife of the then military governor of Oyo State, Mrs Kehinde Olurin, conference secretaries, representatives of the different church denominations, relatives, friends from far and near, the General Secretary of the Baptist Convention and so many other dignitaries witnessed the ceremony. It was a great day for my family and I. So many people who had worked with me and who had the opportunity paid glowing tributes to our work and to what God had achieved through my wife and I, in our over three decades of service to the Convention. In one of the tributes, the General Secretary of the Convention was happy to say that I was never found guilty of the three W's – Wealth, Women and Wine. It was a day of joy for me and for my family as well.

The Public Call (Civil Service Commissioner, Ondo State)

> "...Do here in your home, what we have heard you did in Capernaum."
>
> *Luke 4:23*

After my retirement, I devoted much of my time and energy to writing, and, once in a while, visiting other places. I did that until the military government in Ondo State invited me to serve as a commissioner in the civil service of the State in 1987. The appointment came as a surprise to us. I was away in Ilorin to see my sister Sarah when the news was broken to us. My daughter, Kemi, and I, were on our way out one morning when we met a family friend who was so excited to see us that he could not even acknowledge our greetings. All he wanted to do at that moment was to confirm what he had heard, which to us, was still unknown. When we told him we were not aware of what was happening, he broke the news to us that I had been appointed as a commissioner in the civil service. He said the news was on radio and television and that the Ondo State government was looking for me. Not long after we heard the news, the government confirmed the appointment to me formally through a letter, and it became a thing of joy to everyone in the family and the Baptist Convention.

Since we did not prepare for the appointment, we had a little hitch moving some of our belongings to Akure. I was very worried but my worry did not last long because the Ondo State government stepped in and took charge of our movement. The government provided us with official quarters and a few days after we moved into the quarters, the swearing-in took place and I began work immediately.

I was not the only appointee, three other people were also appointed but they were sworn in few months before I was appointed. Dr. Ogunmilade was a lecturer at Obafemi Awolowo University, Rev. Alokan was a minister and principal of a grammar school and Ambassador Akadiri had been an ambassador of Nigeria to London and Canada before he retired to Akure. Much later, the government appointed two other people into two other commissions. I had a great time serving the people of Ondo State, most especially because with God's help and family support, I combined my work as a commissioner with my pastoral work.

Though I was retired, I still preached at every opportunity because I could not imagine myself abandoning God's work. Nevertheless, I tried the best I could to serve the people, the state and the nation. One of the good things about the appointment was that it helped us in the completion of the various projects we were undertaking in Igbara-Oke, such as the Nursery/Primary school. My wife was the chairman of the building committee and she worked tirelessly to make sure the project came to reality. When the project was finally completed, it was suggested that it should be named after me but I humbly declined. Even when inter-house sports competition began in the school and sport houses were to be named after some of us, I turned down the offer. Humility is one lesson I learnt in my journey through life. I also learnt so many lessons while I was serving in government. One of them is that you can be in government and genuinely serve the people without enriching your purse or cutting corners.

I made sure I was plain in all my official and personal dealings because I could not allow the family name that God had helped me to build over the years, to be soiled by any untoward act. The other commissioners too tried their best to make sure that they served diligently. Later in 1991, I was aided by the government to go to Singapore for a leadership course and the trip accorded me the opportunity to look at areas of life in the country that could be duplicated in Ondo State. It was indeed an eye-opener for me because my ideas about service and leadership was enormously enhanced. Apart from doing the government work, I was also appointed to serve as adviser to the Ondo Baptist Association which I served for six years. During those years, I made my contribution towards the growth of all the churches in the conferences, my home town, all the Baptist churches and other Christian bodies.

Even before retirement, I had always been a stickler for thrift spending and that long-nurtured attitude was what I fell back on after I retired from active religious and public duties. After my retirement, I fell back on my pension, the houses I built and my savings. Following the advice of one of my friends, Param, I took up a life insurance policy with Northern Assurance in 1961 and I insured my life with the firm for 19 years.

After 19 years and nothing happened, the firm paid me my premium and it was from the money that we bought a house in Ibadan. I learnt in my youth that no matter how small any amount of money was, there was something I could do with it. My wife and I were also able to build another house in Igbara-Oke with our savings and the proceeds from the rents are a good source of income in retirement. The pension I receive from government has been helping in taking care of some of the things I need to do. In addition, the children have not been shirking in their responsibilities.

I have found writing a great source of joy before and after my retirement. I have written seven books and I am planning to write more, particularly devotional books and Christian books. The first two books I wrote while in active service were written to help the course of Christianity. I wrote the book, *The Seven Words on the Cross,* for people to appreciate the special and crucial time of our Lord Jesus Christ on the cross before He died for the sins of humanity. I published *1001 Bible Questions and Answers* immediately I retired from public service, to help the faith of growing Christians and, gladly, many people who have read the book have continued to tell me of how much it has impacted on their lives. *The 12 Apostles* was written to chronicle the life, time and works of outstanding apostles in the Bible. My love for singing also led me to write a book about religious hymns. I carried out a research into what prompted the church hymns and found out that they were written and composed based on bible teachings. Religious hymns mean a lot to me because of the soulful messages and power they convey and I have continued to pray that hymns remain a good part of our service to God in the Church and anywhere the Christian faith is professed.

Many people have misconceptions about who the church is or what a church should be. Our Lord Jesus Christ, when He was coming to the world was not charged by God to build church structures. We are the church and not the building, therefore, as Christians, we need to emphasize that to have eternal life calls for knowing and accepting Jesus Christ as one's Lord and Saviour, which should be reflected in our hearts and actions, since our body represents the church. Some people have also brought division into the Body of Christ by dwelling so much on denomination. That some of us belong to the Anglican, Baptist, Catholic and Pentecostal churches does not make us different from one another. The bottom-line of Christianity is that there is only one church, one faith and one Lord (Ephesians 4:5). John 3:16 says, "For God so loved the world that He gave His only begotten son that whosoever believes in him would not perish but have everlasting life." Our denomination is of less importance to God; rather, it is our dedication and righteousness to His words that count. Though our tongues and tribes differ, we should strive to ignore those things that divide us and stress more on the many things that bind us. We should see ourselves as one big, but indivisible entity, in the Body of Christ. Even in retirement, I have continued to advocate that the church of Christ must be portrayed as one!

Meeting other Civil Service Commissioners

25th Wedding Anniversary

Retirement Service @ Bodija Estate Baptist Church, Ibadan 1986:

Grace and Mrs Kehinde Olurin

At some of our children's wedding

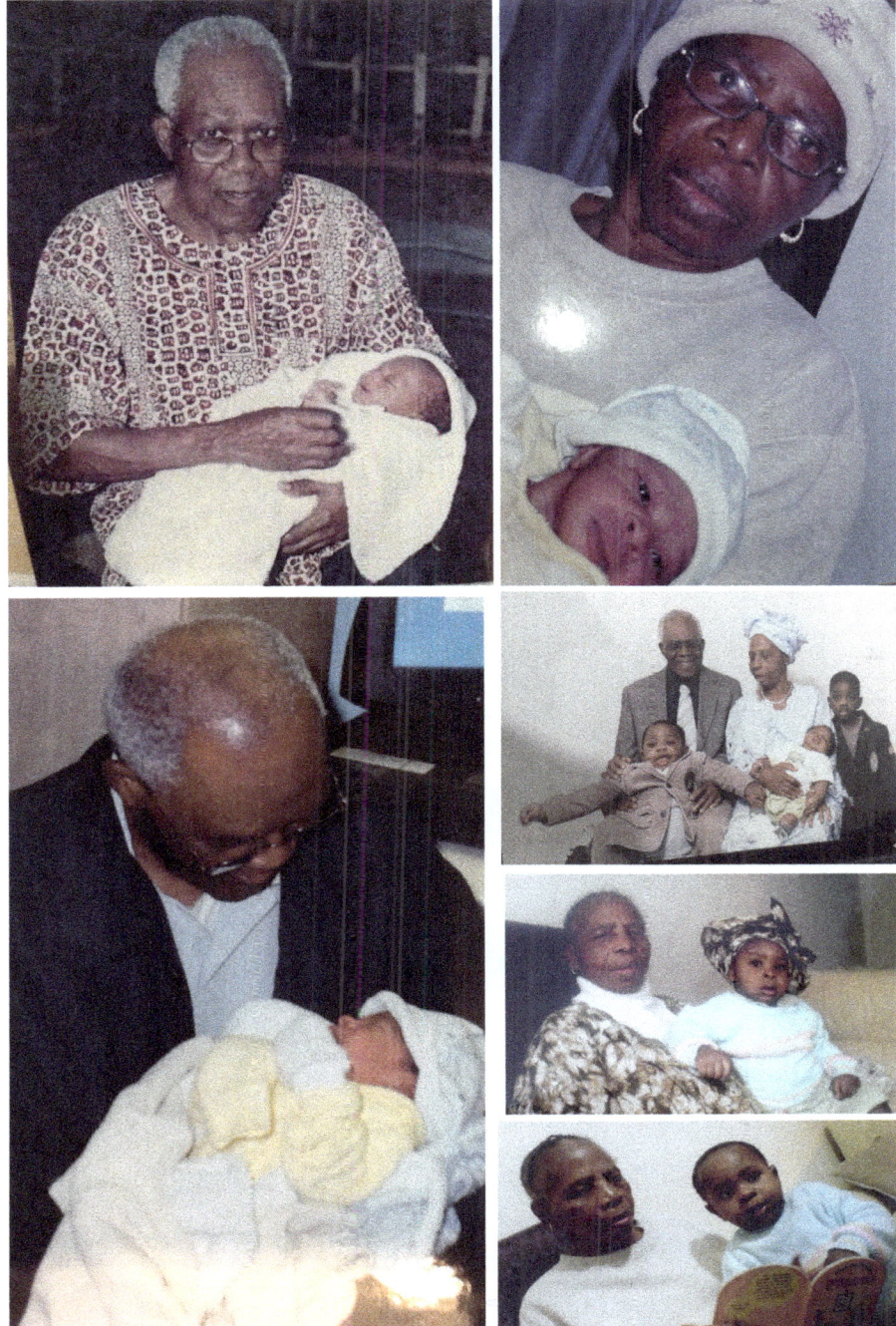

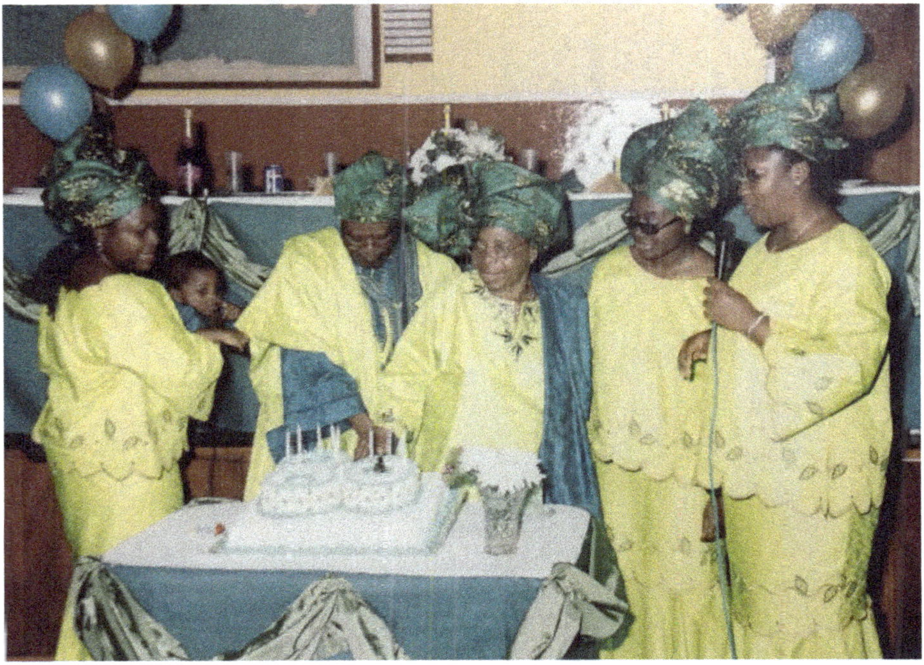

50th Wedding Anniversary

Mexico 2012

CHAPTER TEN

SOJOURNER IN ENGLAND

*"And we know that all things work together for good to those who love God, to those who are the called according to **His** purpose".*

- Romans 8:28

Sometime in 2000, our children arranged that their mother and I go to England to visit our daughter, Kemi. Before the trip though, my wife suddenly fell ill and after her initial treatment at the General Hospital, Akure, she was transferred to the Lagos University Teaching Hospital, General Hospital, Ikeja and later Motayo Hospital, Ikeja. When she fully recovered from the sickness, we set out for the trip to England on August 26, 2000 aboard a British Airways plane. While on board in the air and, halfway between Lagos and London, another terrible sickness hit my wife. This time around, it was devastating.

She did not show any sign of sickness before we boarded the plane so it was a shock to me when it happened. She was given oxygen by a doctor on board. While he tried his best to keep her alive, the cabin crew too swung into action by sending a message to the airport in London that there was a medical emergency on board and a medical team should be placed on standby to take my wife to the hospital. All I could do, and did, was to call on Jesus in the midst of my wife's illness. Once the plane touched down, the medical personnel immediately came on board. They took my wife from her seat, strapped her into a stretcher and wheeled her out of the plane into a waiting ambulance. At that moment, many thoughts ran riot in my mind and I could not fathom why the incident happened when it did and the way it did. While I was still trying to come to terms with what was happening, one of the medical personnel walked up to me and gave me the name and address of the hospital where my wife was being taken to. A few minutes later, another official came to tell me that he would lead me through immigration to avoid unnecessary delays.

Meanwhile, Kemi was waiting to meet us at the airport already. When I came out of the arrival lounge and she did not see her mother, she looked surprised and, naturally, asked after her. I told her what happened and that her mother had been taken to the named hospital. She was shocked but I managed to calm her down as we took a taxi to the hospital. My wife was given some emergency treatment and Kemi was advised to get her to the GP the following week as it was a bank holiday weekend. My wife took ill again two days later and she was taken to the nearest hospital where she spent eight months and four days on admission. When she was not recovering as fast as we wanted, we applied to the hospital for her to be discharged and taken to Kemi's home for closer monitoring. After many tough administrative challenges and battles and, satisfied that she could be treated at home, the doctors discharged her and gave us the necessary equipment and medications for her treatment. Her health was to be monitored by our general practitioner. We did have some help for few hours daily and Kemi and I took charge of the remaining hours.

During that tough period, I could not question God's purpose for what happened, I could only ask why it happened while we were mid-air, and on board an airplane but, in it all, God is sovereign and He answers to no man. The incident was like a dream to me but I thank God for the children because they have been supportive in every way. My wife and I only planned to stay in England for a few weeks but considering her state of health, we could not return to Nigeria. Permission to change our status was applied for and it was granted. My wife's health improved tremendously from then on and we were able to move on with our lives, albeit, far away from Nigeria.

Grace has been wonderful through it all and I thank God for giving me the opportunity to know her. It was because of her support and open heart that we were able to achieve most of the things we achieved. Never for once did I think otherwise about my marriage to her because of her good nature and love for me. Our love has been sincere and it will remain so. My advice to people is that if you want to live a good life, you ought to have love in your heart. Love is the greatest commandment and it was what Jesus Christ lived and died for. With God's help, my wife and I have moved on with life in England and we are not regretting anything. Rather, I have taken advantage of the opportunity that our sojourn in England has provided for me.

One of those advantages was the computer literacy programme introduced by the British government for senior citizens. The programme was free and you went for lectures at your own convenience. Computer centres were set up all across London so that you could go to anyone nearest your home or place of work to learn. The programme was very easy because we were taught with modern learning aids and after the programme, participants were issued with a City of Guild Certificate in

Adult Literacy. To my amazement, I became the focus of a newspaper article titled "**Age is No Barrier**" in *The South London Press* edition of September 7, 2004. The story brought so much attention to me that whenever I went out during that period, people stopped me on the way to congratulate and commend me on my zeal to acquire more education, at my age. To me, what I did was not extra-ordinary, all I wanted to do was move with the times so that I would not be left behind in the computer age. I wish the programme could be replicated in Nigeria, so that the elderly in the society can benefit from the information age. The programme showed me that the better enlightened people are, the better for the society.

I am so grateful to God for my wife and the good children He gave us. Like Joshua, I gratefully say, "As for me and my house, we will serve the Lord" **(Joshua 24:15)**. I am thankful to God also, for the good people I came across in my journeys through life. They guided, blessed and helped me at every significant crossroad and milestone of my life endeavours. They assisted me to scale every hurdle and accomplish all of my set goals and objectives.

I thank God for Venerable S.O. Akinluyi, the headmaster of St. Paul's Primary school, Igbara- Oke whom God used to convince my father to allow me to go to school. I remember, Bishop Okusanya who brought the Boys' Brigade to Igbara-Oke and taught us to be thrift in our spending, pay our tithes regularly and give with all our hearts. Those lessons have spurred me on till date. I thank Mr. B.O. Falana for accommodating me in their family house in Abeokuta when I had nowhere to stay. Pastor Lawanson was another good man. It was through him that I got the job of at the seminary. My sister, Sarah was another great influence; a woman after God's heart. In the words of Paul, "I thank my God every time I remember you" **(Philippians 1:3 NIV)**. I do not have any regrets meeting these people and numerous others. My heart will continue to pray for all the people who contributed to my life, as long as it keeps beating. I am not resting because I am yet to reach the finish line!

Gains or Rewards of Serving God

The gains of serving God are far too numerous to count. That I have lived this long is one of the gains. When Hezekiah was sick, he cried to God for help and God had mercy on him by adding another fifteen years to his life. When I retired in 1986, all I was earning was a little under ₦1000 per month, but now, I spend more than that in a couple of days. How God is doing it? I do not know and I cannot explain where the extra is coming from. God's promise to me is that I should always depend on Him. True to His word in **Hebrews 6:10**, He has been supplying all my needs according to His riches in glory through Christ Jesus **(Philippians 4:19)**. God never forgets any man's labour and service to Him and His people. What some people may say I lost, I have only gained more abundantly, because God promised me from day one, that I would never lack. He has been fulfilling that promise, therefore I do not entertain any fears. The God that has taken me thus far will surely continue to be with me till the end.

Forever Serving God

> "Expect great things from God; attempt great things for God."
>
> *William Carey (1761-1834)*

It is an erroneous belief that a man or woman who is committed to the service of God retires at one point in time or the other. You do not retire when you are serving God and when you decide to follow Jesus, you go the whole hog. There is no turning back. Life is a race and before you are crowned a winner, you must get to the finish line. I will continue to run till I get to the finish line. Many people believe that when we retire from *official* service, the race is over but that is not the case. It is never over until it is over. The service of God is eternal. For this reason, the race is not over for me. I hope to keep serving God until I inhale my last breath.

My determination to succeed has been one of my major strengths because determination is the foundation for success and I am determined to serve God till the end. The race is not over until one crosses the finish line, which for me, gets closer and closer as each day goes by. I remain grateful to God for everything. Though there have been tough times, God in His infinite mercies has led me safely through them all, and in the midst of those tough times, there have been great times too. I believe that "…in all things, God works for the good of those who love Him." **(Romans 8:28)**. God is ever faithful!

I trust God that at the end of my days, my testimony shall be like that of Apostle Paul who said, "I have fought a good fight, I have finished the race, I have kept the faith…" **(2 Timothy 4:7-8)**. My earnest desire and prayer is that I should have the strength to keep on serving God until He calls me home.
May it be said of me when I am gone, that, like David, "He served the purpose of God in his generation" **(Acts 13:36, NIV)** and may people praise God because of me **(Galatians 1:24 NIV)**. Amen and Amen!

Bowen University, Iwo
Honorary Doctorate Award 2012

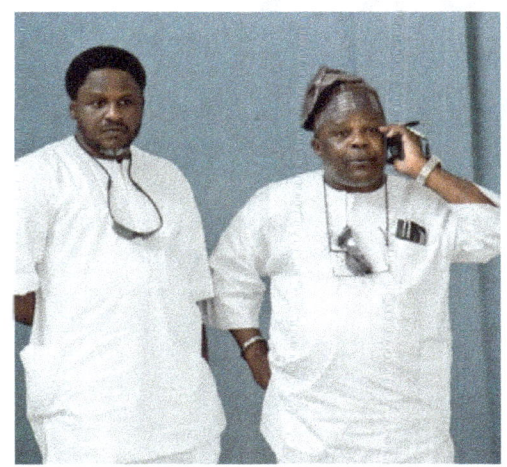

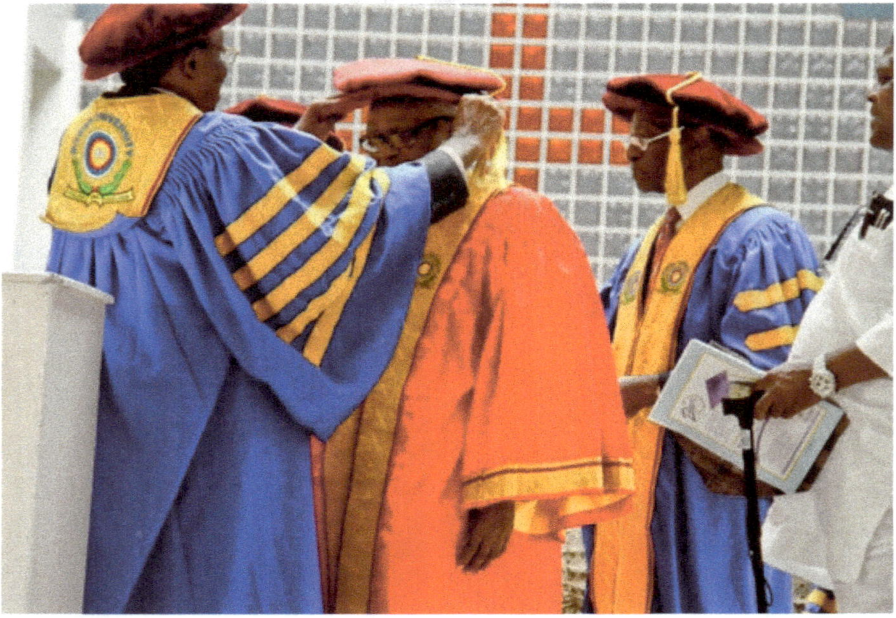

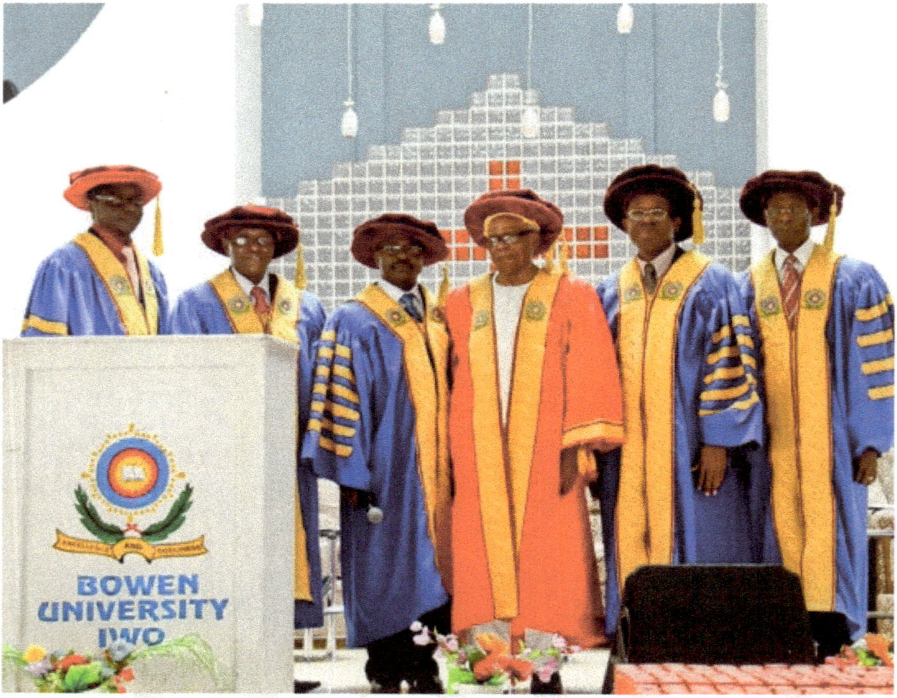
BOWEN
UNIVERSITY
IWO

APPENDIX 1

Letter of Commendation

The American Baptist Mission

Office of
The Headmaster
Telephone No. 88,
P. O. Box 32.

Baptist Boys' High School,
Abeokuta, Nigeria.
April 1, 1949.

<u>TO WHOM IT MAY CONCERN.</u>

    This is to testify that Mr. R. W. O. Ojo was under my direct tuition for a few years and latter on became the librarian in his alma mater. In both capacities, he rendered an all round good of himself. As a proof of his intellectual ability, he left school in Class IV but with private study he was able to pass the Senior Cambridge Examination after a year. He is respectful and industrious.
    I heartily recommend him for the best consideration you can give a young man of age and experience.

E. L. Akisanya
HEADMASTER BAPTIST BOYS
ABEOKUTA.

APPENDIX 2

Certificate of Service

NIGERIAN RAILWAY

Certificate of Service

This certificate is given without alteration or erasure of any kind

Staff (Mech). Department   January 1953.

I hereby certify that William Rufus Olatunji Ojo was employed in the service of the Nigerian Railway in the several capacities and for the several periods of time specified below:—

Date entered Service: 6th July 1948.

Rank on entering: Temporary Clerk.

Subsequent Promotions: 3rd Class Clerk.

Latest Position: 3rd Class Clerk.

Date of leaving Service: 23rd January 1952.

Salary or wage at date of leaving Service: £96 per annum.

Ability: G O O D.

Conduct during Service: G O O D.

Cause of leaving: Resignation.

Head of Department
CHIEF ESTABLISHMENT OFFICER.

General Manager

Signature of Employee:

The holder is advised that no guarantee can be given that this certificate will be replaced, if lost by him.

APPENDIX 3

Certificate of Ordination

Nigerian Baptist Convention
Certificate of Ordination

We, the undersigned, hereby certify that upon the recommendation and request of the First Baptist Igede Baptist Church at Igede which had full and sufficient opportunity for judging of his gifts, and after satisfactory examination by us in regard to his Christian experience, call to the ministry, and views of Bible Doctrine,

W. R. O. Ojo

was solemnly and publicly ordained to the work of The Gospel Ministry at Igede, on the 13th day of October, 1957.

Ordaining Council: S. Maurryn, CHAIRMAN

R. L. West, SECRETARY

J. T. Ayorinde

T. N. Patterson

J. C. Pool

Sam M. Lawton

APPENDIX 4

Farewell Address from 1st Baptist Church Igede - Ekiti

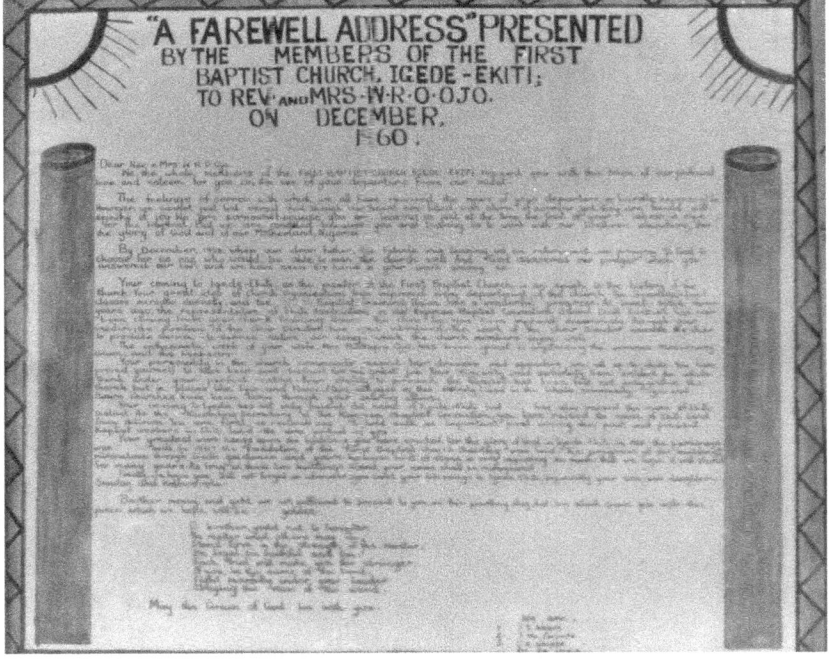

APPENDIX 5

Convention Award

https://en.wikipedia.org/wiki/Nigerian_Baptist_Convention

APPENDIX 6

University Certificates

https://www.wfu.edu
https://en.wikipedia.org/wiki/Wake_Forest_University

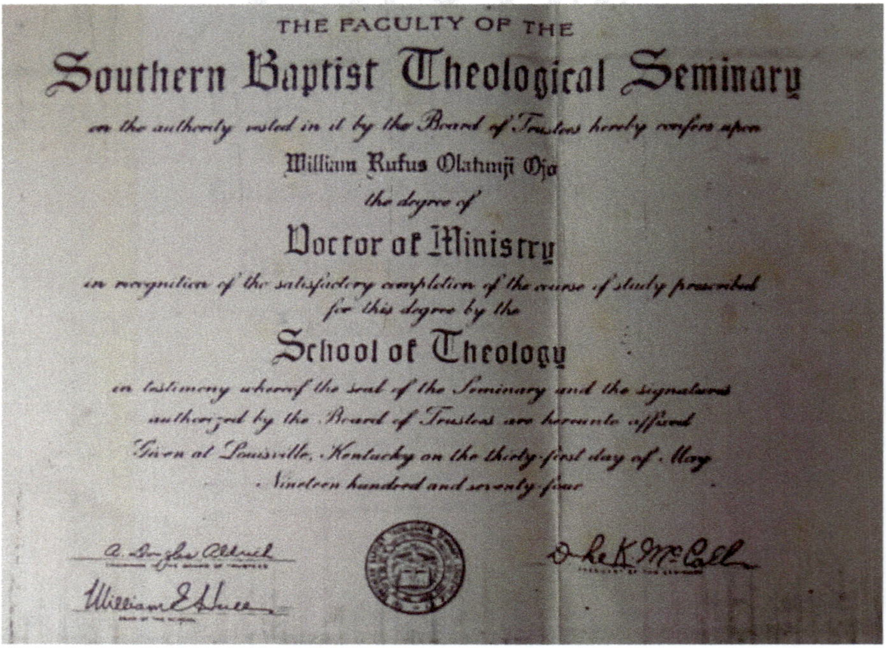

THE FACULTY OF THE
Southern Baptist Theological Seminary

on the authority vested in it by the Board of Trustees hereby confers upon

William Rufus Olatunji Oja

the degree of

Doctor of Ministry

in recognition of the satisfactory completion of the course of study prescribed for this degree by the

School of Theology

in testimony whereof the seal of the Seminary and the signatures authorized by the Board of Trustees are hereunto affixed. Given at Louisville, Kentucky on the thirty-first day of May Nineteen hundred and seventy-four

https://www.sbts.edu
https://en.wikipedia.org/wiki/Southern_Baptist_Theological_Seminary

APPENDIX 7

ADULT EDUCATION DEPARTMENT
OF THE
NIGERIAN BAPTIST CONVENTION

Certificate of Appreciation

AWARDED TO

THE REV. DR. W. R. OLA. OJO

in appreciation for his/her special services
in the fight against adult illiteracy.

Date AUGUST 30, 1987

Secretary, Adult Education Department
Nigerian Baptist Convention.

BAPTIST PRESS (NIG.) LTD., IBADAN.

APPENDIX 8

NBC Certificate of Meritorious Service

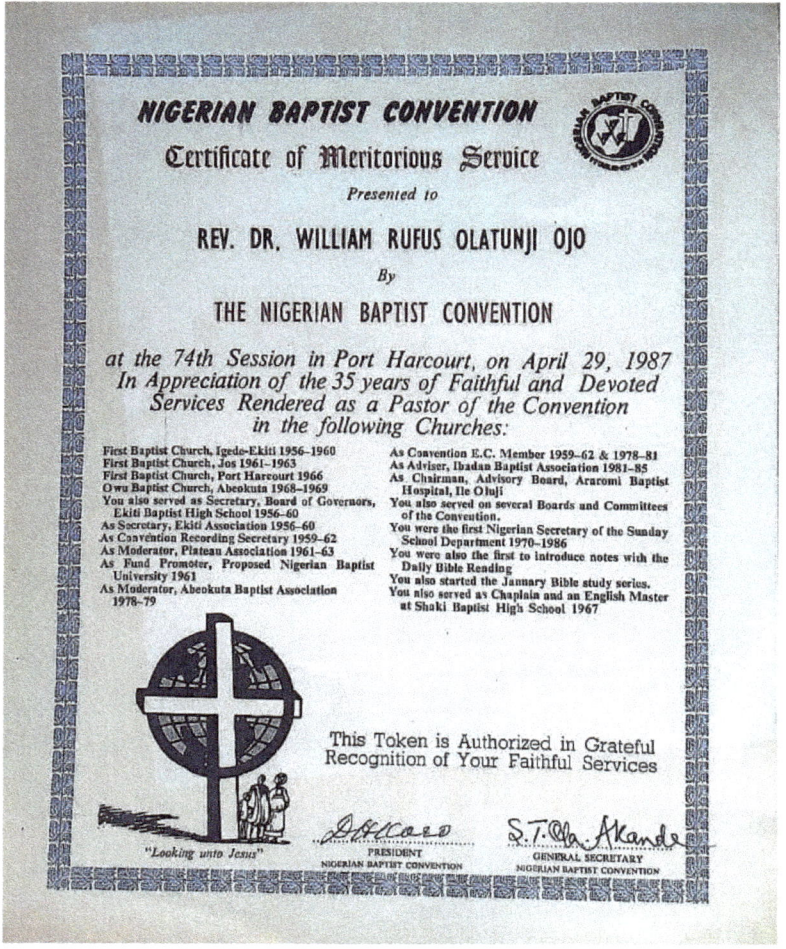

https://en.wikipedia.org/wiki/Nigerian_Baptist_Convention

APPENDIX 9

Haggai Institute Advanced Leadership Training Certificate

APPENDIX 10

14 South London Press, Tuesday, September 7, 2004

News

IN BRIEF

Centre campaign to march on town hall

LADYWELL: The campaign to save Ladywell Leisure Centre will march on Lewisham Town Hall a week tomorrow. Protesters opposed to the bulldozing of the pool to make way for a secondary school will join forces with parents who believe the school should be in the north of the borough in the Deptford and New Cross areas.

They will march from the leisure centre at 6pm before joining the full council meeting where Local Education Action by Parents (LEAP) councillor Helen Le Fevre will hand over a 3,000-strong petition.

Liberal Democrat councillor Julia Fletcher will then put forward a motion calling for the demolition of the pool to be delayed until a replacement is created.

CORDON: police close off Streatham Mews
Photo: PETER HARRISON/8329/1/S

Man injured in fight

STREATHAM: A man was taken to hospital with a gash to the nose after he was involved in a fight in Streatham High Road on Friday. The incident happened at 3pm as shoppers enjoyed the afternoon sun. Witnesses said they saw four men fighting before one produced what appeared to be a knife.

One of the men stumbled to the ground covered in blood, his shirt ripped off and the others ran away in the direction of Streatham Mews, just off the high street.

Floodlit pitch petition

EAST DULWICH: A girls' school has upset neighbours with plans to build a floodlit artificial grass pitch next to its sports field.

James Allen's Girls' School in East Dulwich Grove plans to extend its existing 4.7 hectare sports field with a 100m by 67m pitch.

Neighbours signed a 22-strong petition opposing the pitch because of the bright lights and high fencing.

But planners at Southwark council are expected to grant permission for the proposed pitch tonight.

Pupil numbers decision

BROCKLEY: Councillors have been asked to agree a reduction in the number of pupils entering Brockley Primary School.

They will decide at tomorrow night's mayor and cabinet meeting whether to reduce the intake of the Brockley Road school from 60 to 30, starting in September 2005.

The reason for the change is a lack of demand for places.

Affordable housing demand for plans

A SWANKY housing scheme complete with wine bar will have to include an exceptionally high number of affordable homes.

Developer London Quadrant says 76 per cent of its 122-flat scheme earmarked for Rye Lane will be competitively priced.

The percentage is well above Mayor Ken Livingstone's guideline of 50 per cent – designed to help key workers such as nurses and teachers.

Tonight Southwark's planning committee is expected to agree the Rye Lane scheme subject to a number of conditions listed as part of a section 106 agreement between the council and the developer.

The scheme proposes 122 flats with 56 basement parking spaces on the site at the junction of Rye Lane and Heaton Road.

Blocks would look on to a central courtyard and would include shops and a cafe and wine bar.

A second application proposes redeveloping existing council offices on Heaton Road into a 22-flat block. This would also boast landscaping and shops.

In December last year, the planning committee granted permission providing that developers enter into a special agreement.

Under the 106 agreement Southwark requires the development to contain high proportion affordable housing. The council also wants developers to spend £75,000 on improvements to the junction of Rye Lane and Heaton Road.

It also wants £10,000 towards funding a part-time worker in the Peckham Town Centre management group.

'Age is no barrier'

KEYS TO LEARNING: William Ojo, centre, with Helen Harmony and Burhan Grozia of Learn Direct
Photo: GEORGINA COOK/19800/3/S

By KEELY SHERBIRD

WHEN William Ojo was born in Nigeria 78 years ago few people had telephones and televisions were a far away fantasy.

Now as the new school term begins and youngsters trudge back to classes the Lewisham pensioner is returning to continue his studies using the latest communications technology.

The retired preacher completed a City and Guilds certificate in adult literacy at Lewisham College and still visits the college regularly.

He said: "Age is not a barrier – people should continue to learn and expand their horizons and knowledge as long as they live.

"I had never had the opportunity to use a computer before so I started it from the beginners course then continued on.

"Now I'm able to use the email, do research and get the BBC news on the internet."

For further information on adult courses call 020 8692 0353.

Man in dock over parkland shooting

AN ALLEGED gunman accused of shooting dead a 21-year-old man has appeared in court.

Marlon Stubbs, 23, is charged with the murder of Adrian Marriott in Brixton on June 9. Mr Marriott was found with bullet wounds to the face in parkland near Barrington Road just after 9am. Paramedics pronounced him dead at the scene.

Stubbs, of Ward Point, Kennington, spoke only to confirm his name at the plea and directions hearing at the Old Bailey, which was adjourned until October 28.

He did not enter a plea to the charge of murder and was remanded in custody by the Common Serjeant of London, Judge Peter Beaumont.

A second man has already been charged with the attack and will appear at the Old Bailey for a plea and directions hearing on September 24.

APPENDIX 11

POST HONORARY DOCTORATE AWARD SPEECH

With a heart of gratitude to God, I receive this award and dedicate it to God and to my wife - Grace.

- I appreciate immensely the Governing council and Senate of this University, whom has thought me fit for this award.
- I am also grateful to The Vice Chancellor, Prof. Olagbenro and his team for the great work that is been done here.
- To, my friends and families, who have come from far and near to celebrate with me. I say you will be sent for in high places.

Jeremiah 1 verse 5 says *"Before thou camest forth out of the womb I sanctified thee and ordained thee"* (KJV)

- I was born in a little town called Igbara-Oke.
- Unlike most people, I was not opportune to know my mother nor was I ever shown my mum's look alike.
- My father always took me to the farm with him.
- One day coming from the farm with my father, we ran into to the headmaster by name Mr. S.O Akinluyi.
- The headmaster queried my father as to why I was not enrolled in school.
- After some persuasion, my father finally agreed to let me start school the following year.
- Mr. Akinluyi still would not agree until my father finally consented to me starting the following school term.
- So my life's journey began.

Psalms 37 verse 23 says God orders the steps of the righteous.
- Though I was born and raised as an Anglican,
- I was not able to get admission to the renowned St Andrews College Oyo because my father was a polygamist.
- This led me to the great Baptist Boys High School (BBHS Abeokuta).
- Due to financial constraints, I dropped out after 3 years instead of spending the required six years.
- I worked as the first paid BBHS school librarian and studied for Cambridge on my own.
- With God's help, I was able to pass my Cambridge examination in flying colors with exemption from London matriculation.
- After passing my exams, I got a job with the Electricity Corporation in Lagos.
- I later joined Nigeria Railway Corporation and then The Call to the ministry came.

The Call
- I took the call to the ministry with excitement but it came with some cost, one of which was my loosing my then girlfriend who did not want to marry a pastor.
- God graciously led me to marry Grace my wife some years later. Looking back now after 57years of marriage, I could not have had a better wife and companion.

Other calls to the Masters service came, such as:
- Becoming The1st Nigerian Recording Secretary for the Baptist Convention.

- Being chosen by the Nigerian Baptist Convention to become the principal promoter and fund raiser for the then proposed Baptist University now Bowen University.
- Becoming the 1ST Nigerian Sunday School Secretary of the Baptist convention.
- Becoming The Associate Coordinator for the Nigerian Alabama Partnership.
- The Baptist University assignment did not come with an extra income or benefit for me and my family plus,
- I had to travel all around Nigeria and Ghana
- It was a sowing time with a heart for God and His work.
- Thanks be to God, it has not lost its harvest.

Genesis 39 verse 2 says and the Lord was with Joseph. I too can truly say and the Lord was with William.

- Though I came from a very humble background, though I dropped out of the secondary school and studied on my own, the Lord set me up in high places through the Baptist convention.
- When I retired and was wondering what next, He showed up, He gave me a job as a Commissioner in Ondo state amongst other things.
- When I thought I had been forgotten like Joseph, He remembered me, just like today again.

I submit to you all today that "And I know that ALL things work together for good to them that love God, to them who are called according to His purpose. Like brother Paul, I can say that I fought a good fight and have kept the faith.

2 Corinthians 1 verse 4 says "who encourages us in all our tribulations, that we may be able to encourage them which are in any trouble"

- I have enjoyed the blessings and favor of God.
- The Nigerian Baptist Convention invested in me without discriminating.
- In the spirit of encouraging others, my wife and I are setting up "Grace William Foundation". God helping us we intend to donate 1million Naira every year to 10 Bowen University deserving students in dire need of financial assistance.
- The details are been discussed with the Bowen University authority.

In closing, I will like you all to rise and sing with me
This is my story this is my song
Praising my Savior all the day long
This is my story, this is my song
Praising my Savior
All the day Long.

God bless Nigeria.
God bless the Nigerian Baptist Convention.
God bless Bowen University.
God bless you All.
Thank you for coming and I wish you God's journey mercies to your homes.

APPENDIX I2

Newspaper Interview

https://www.ghanamma.com/2012/11/11/bowen-honour-for-the-doyen/

Bowen honour for the Doyen

November 11, 2012

THOUGH his fingers are frail, his body weak and giving him tough time every now and then, but the mind of 89-year old Reverend (Dr.) William Rufus Olatunji Ojo (WRO) is still sound. His memory is still sharp. The man, who last weekend, received an honorary doctorate degree from the Bowen University, Iwo, still remembers vividly his commission as a reverend gentleman of the Baptist Convention. With his back arched, Reverend Ojo sits transfixed for a few seconds, almost watching the narrative footage of his calling in his mind eye. Lowering his voice to tiny whispers, he tells his guest, *"it is something I cannot express. I thank God and I feel honoured that at my age, people will still think that I deserve such an award and I'm very grateful to everybody that has contributed in one way or the other for this."*

He adds, *"just two other persons had been privileged to be so honoured with this award by the school. They are Chief Olusegun Obasanjo and Mr. Gamaliel Onosode."*

The award is in recognition of the octogenarian's immense services to humanity, the Nigerian nation, and invaluable contribution to the progress of the Nigerian Baptist Convention in particular and Christendom in general.

He was part of the initial efforts in the 1960s to raise funds for the take off of the university. He was at Jos then. Between June and December 1961, he was on the road, travelling all over Nigeria and Ghana; Ghana was part of the Nigerian Baptist Convention then. His task was to raise funds in all the churches for the 10 percent contribution of the Nigerian Baptist Convention for the university's take off. The 90 percent was to be provided by the global church.

He stands up from his chair, feeling his shoe sink deep into the rugs, he enthuses, *"I've always believed in doing the Lord's will. Whatever opportunity that came, I will take it."*

One sure way to know a happy man is to look below his eyes, and perhaps, count the number of lines there. Each line, like Unoka's on the wall in Things Fall Apart by Chinua Achebe, represents the weight of his challenges. And what greater gift can a man have than young looks. Even at old age.

Wearing a smile, which glistens, he breathes heavily, *"it is the Lord Himself that made it possible to serve Him. I'm happy when I serve the Lord, and considering what he has done in my life and that of other people, I can't but serve him."*

He says, at a young age, he was determined to excel. He wanted to be educated, but he didn't start school early. With a limitless supply of grit and drive, he has ensured that his dreams did not evaporate. "My father actually was responsible for my late going to school. Every year he had one excuse or the other not to allow me start school. I actually started school at age 11. He normally said he needed somebody to keep his company and to send on errand," he says.

Ojo attended a primary school in his hometown of Igbara Oke, Ondo State. He passes out in 1941. *"There were three of us who did extremely well in the final exams and we were immediately given employment as teachers. I was posted to Ogotun Ekiti. I served there for two years after which I was transferred back to my town for another one year."*

He secured admission to Baptist Boys High School (BBHS), Abeokuta for his secondary education, after failing to gain admission to St Andrews College, Oyo because it is an Anglican school and preference was given to students with Anglican parentage. "Somebody mentioned it to me that BBHS could admit me on merit and I wrote the examination, I passed and was offered admission," he says. Unfortunately, he had to stop in the fourth form because his parents couldn't sponsor his education further. He had earlier sold his bicycle to see the young WRO through primary education.

"At that time, there were only three people who had bicycles in my hometown," he says, sensitively. But God was really kind to WRO, because the principal of the school then, having seen his predicament, decided to help, by giving him employment me as the school's first paid librarian.

"Each time my classmates, who by then had graduated to class five, came to the library, I usually asked for their lesson notes, which I read and digested so well. This coupled with the opportunity of access to countless books in the library, at a point I felt I was sufficiently prepared to sit for the high school exam. I then decided to register as a private candidate for the London Matric Exam at the Abeokuta Grammar School, where Kuti, father of Fela, was the principal. I passed the exam, but didn't have a good grade in English Language, so, I had to resit the subject the following year and I was very excited," he laughs. When he laughs, papa comes out free and young. He notes, eyes hardening and voice inflicting a more serious tone. "After my exams, I was still working in Abeokuta, but later somebody told me that there were opportunities for better remuneration in Lagos. That was how I came to Lagos and was employed in the Electricity Company of Nigeria (ECN). I was in the meter-reading department and it came to a time that I felt the job was not tasking and challenging enough. Later, I moved to Railway at Ebute Metta. I was leaving at Surulere at this time.

GOING into the Ministry?
He enthuses, "I was leaving some houses away from a Baptist Church at Surulere. Because of my background with the Baptist Church all along, it was easy for me to be integrated to the church at Surulere. With my background and experience, it was easy for the Reverend in the church to unearth my potential. I was involved deeply in almost all the aspects of the church, especially Sunday school. Anytime, the Reverend wasn't around, he was always handing the affairs of the church to me. I got so engrossed with this service in the church that it was just a matter of time when I would become a full time minister. I eventually spent for years at Baptist Seminary, Ogbomoso. After which I began my journey of priesthood that took me all around the country."

WRO, as he is fondly called, served the Baptist Mission in Nigeria full- time for close to 40 years, during which time he represented the Convention at various forums around the world.

He was also the Principal Fund Raising Promoter appointed by the Convention to raise funds for the establishment of the Baptist University – a special assignment that took him to every nook and cranny of Nigeria and Ghana in the 1960s. The result of this assignment is the Bowen University, Iwo.

His most memorable experience?
He stands up gently from his chair, feeling his shoe sink deep into the rug, he enthuses, "the day I got married and left home that very day for my first mission in the church in Igede, Ekiti State."

His advice for young couples?
While nodding his head and gurgling with satisfaction, he sighs, "life is

not a bed of roses. The things of the Lord always keep us, so, we should expect the rough and hard times. God will never leave us in that time of difficulty; He will surely come to our rescue. Under every circumstance, we have to love ourselves. Always put God first, your family second and third others. This is the motto I have used. Under every circumstance, I put God first."

What would you predict as Rev. Ojo's routine after retirement?
"Hardwork."
And this seems to have dotted the lines of every page of his life, which he script-edited at age 12: Humane personality. "Retirement doesn't mean that is the end of things. When you retire, you retire into something. You still want to do something at your own convenience and as the Lord has allowed you. Retirement is sometimes a change of life, you can't stay put.

That you're retired does not mean you keep your hands folded of everything. You are ready to face all situations religiously, knowing that no condition is permanent," he says.
At retirement, he was made a Commissioner in the Ondo State Civil Service Commission in Akure in 1987, where he served meritoriously till 1991.
WRO is a motivator, achiever and an author of many books known for his diligence, sense of responsibility, integrity, transparency and achievements.

Other Books by the Author:

- **Eto Isin Aseye Aisun fun Oku Onigbagbo** – *Akojopo Orin ati Bibeli Kika 1986 Baptist Press (Nigeria) Ibadan 7507-7-86-20,000*
- **Stories of Great Hymns** *July 1987 Baptist Press (Nigeria) Ibadan 2,000-10-87-7904*
- **The Twelve Apostles** – *Woleola Printers, Akure*
- **The Seven Words of Jesus on the Cross** *1987– Baptist Press (Nigeria) Ibadan 2,500-6-87-7808*
- **Eto Isin fun Ìsọmọ Tuntun Lórúkọ áti Ìgbọmọ Tuntun Jade** *1991 – Government Printer Akure*
- **1001 Bible Questions and Answers** *November 1999 - Woleola Printers, Akure*

www.ingramcontent.com/pod-product-compliance
Lightning Source LLC
Chambersburg PA
CBHW041957080526
44588CB00021B/2768